Fruit
A Still Life Coloring Book

Illustrations by
Sue-Jen Song

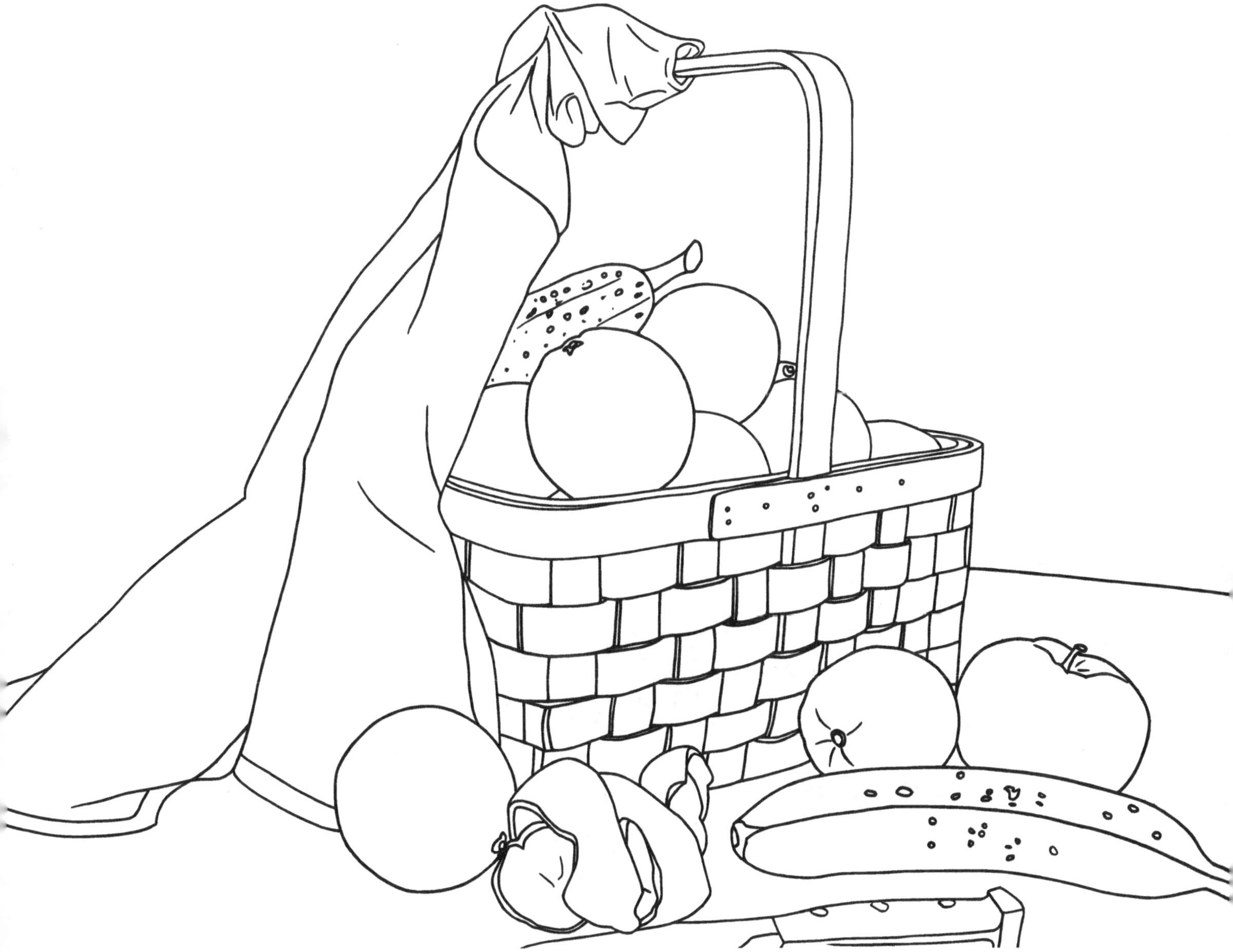

Copyright ©2017 by Sue-Jen Song
All rights reserved.

ISBN: 978-1979577304
First Edition

Printed by CreateSpace, An Amazon.com Company

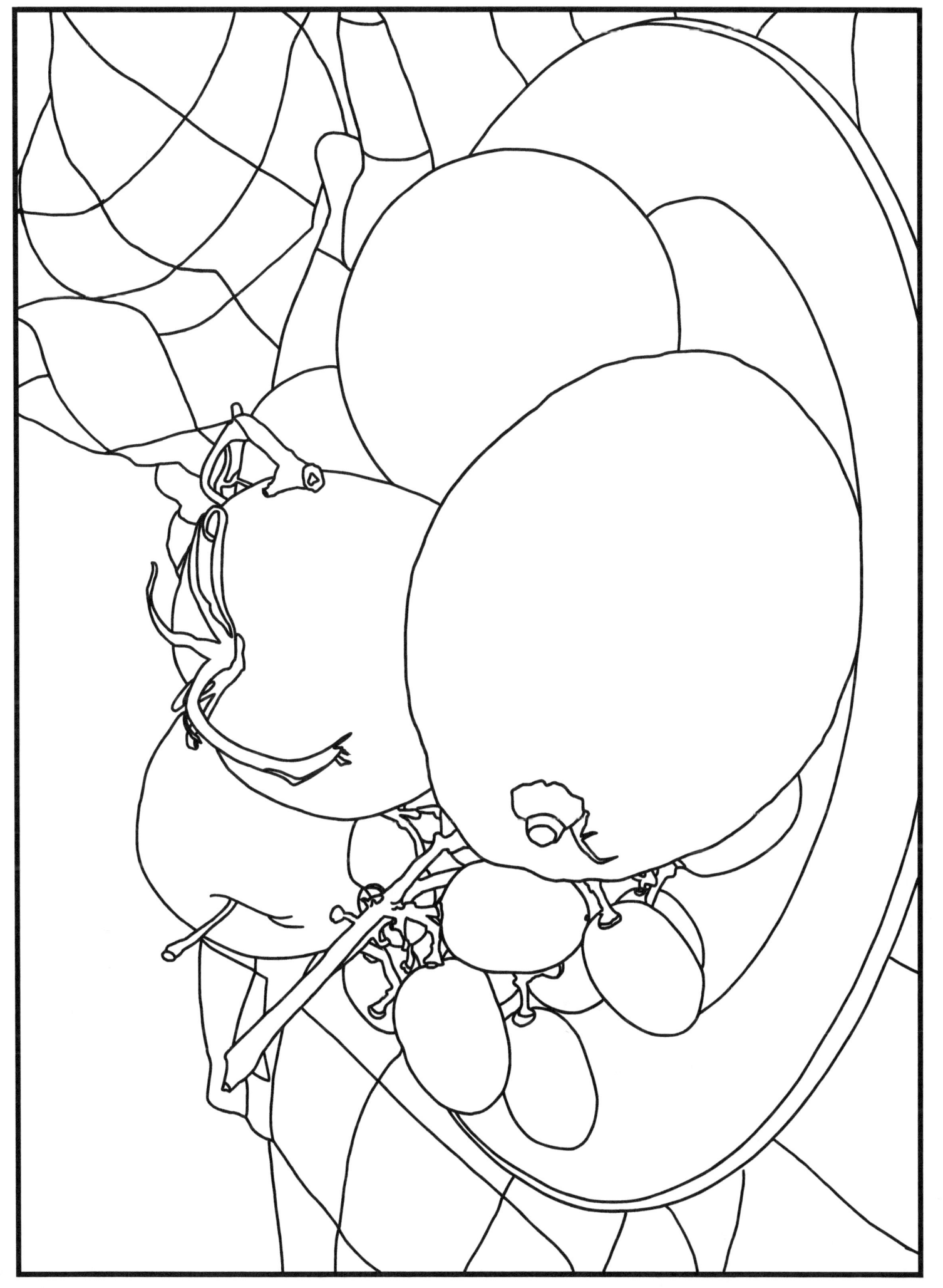

Fruit #1

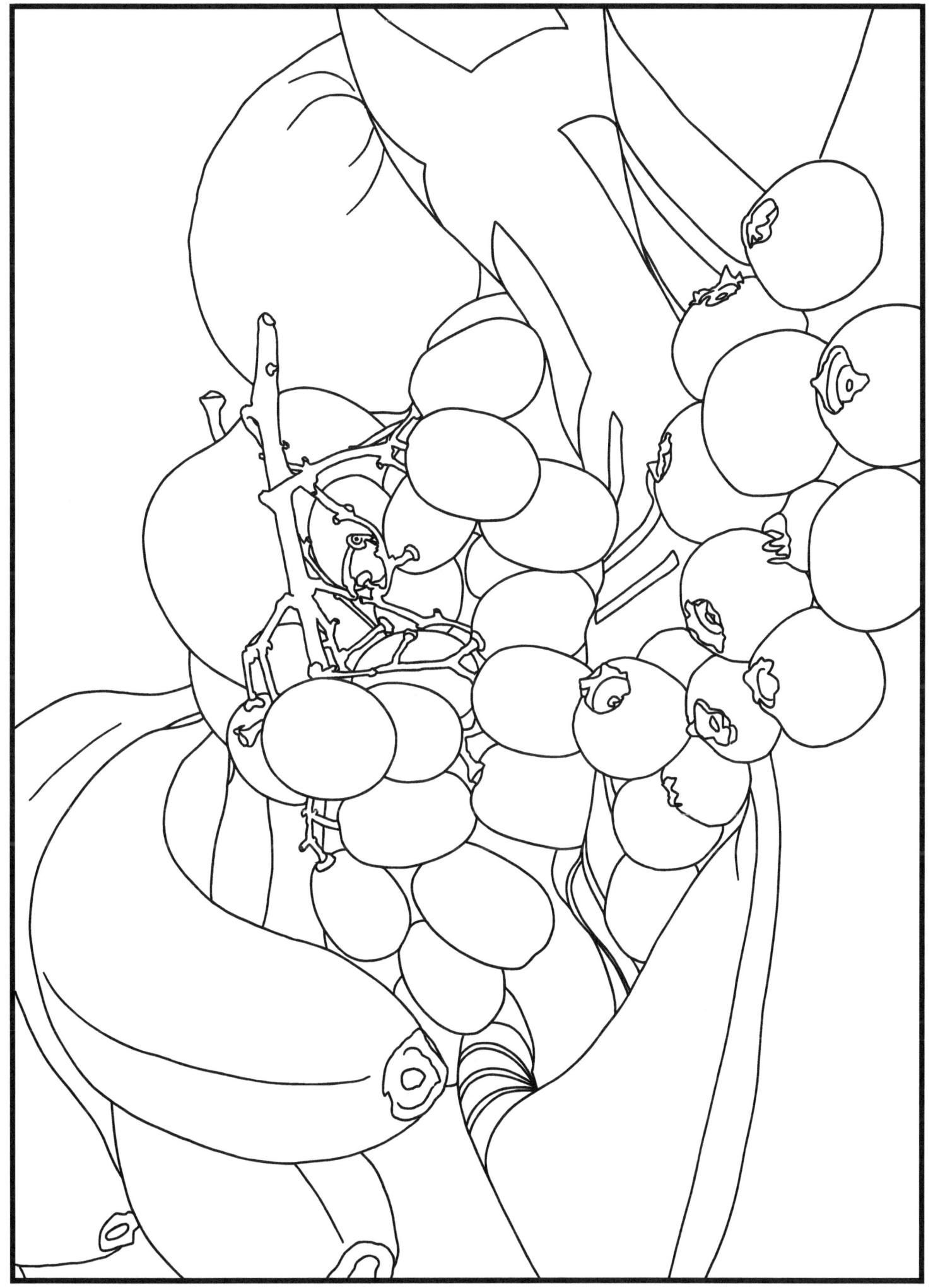

Fruit #2

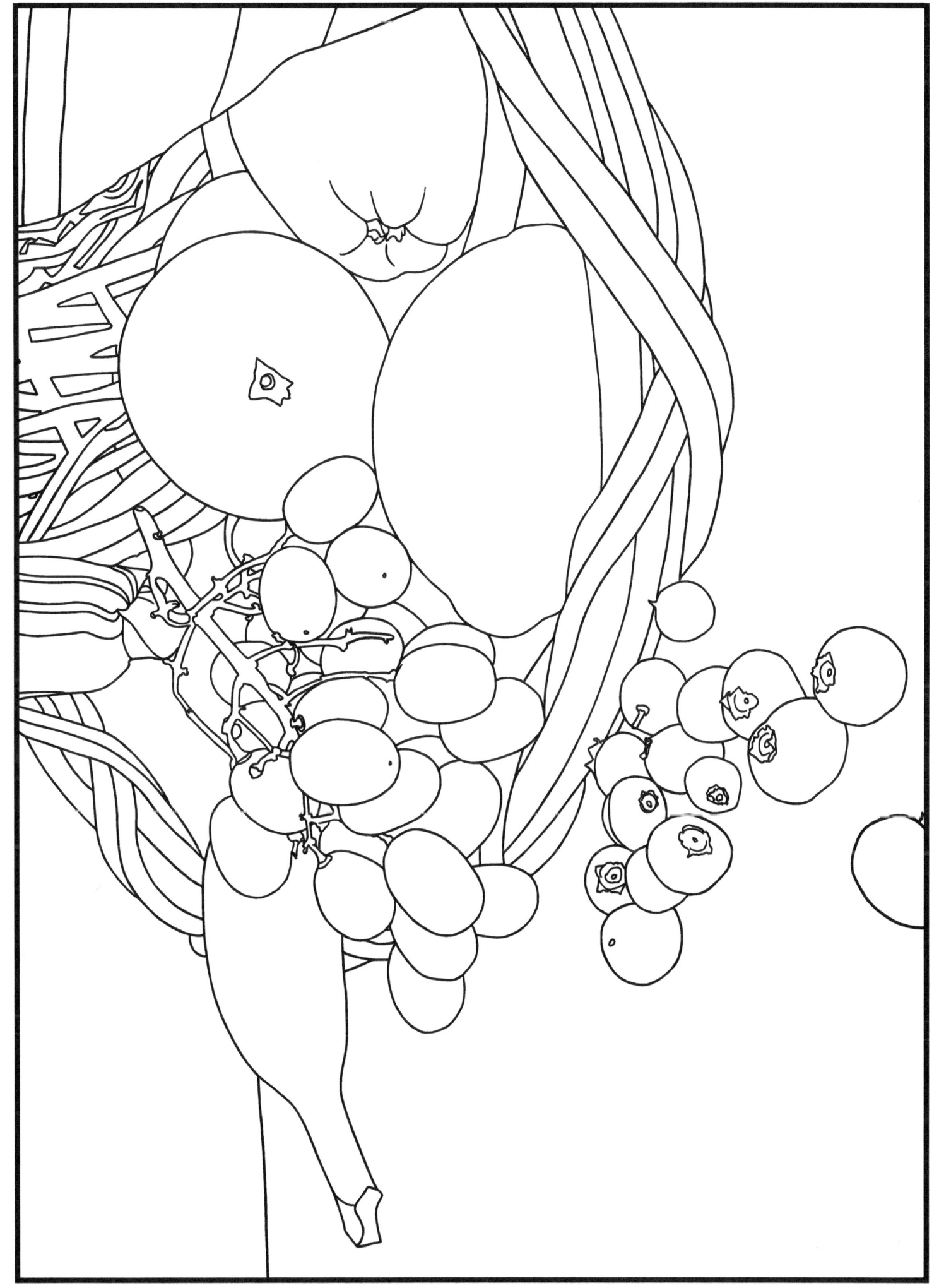

Fruit #3

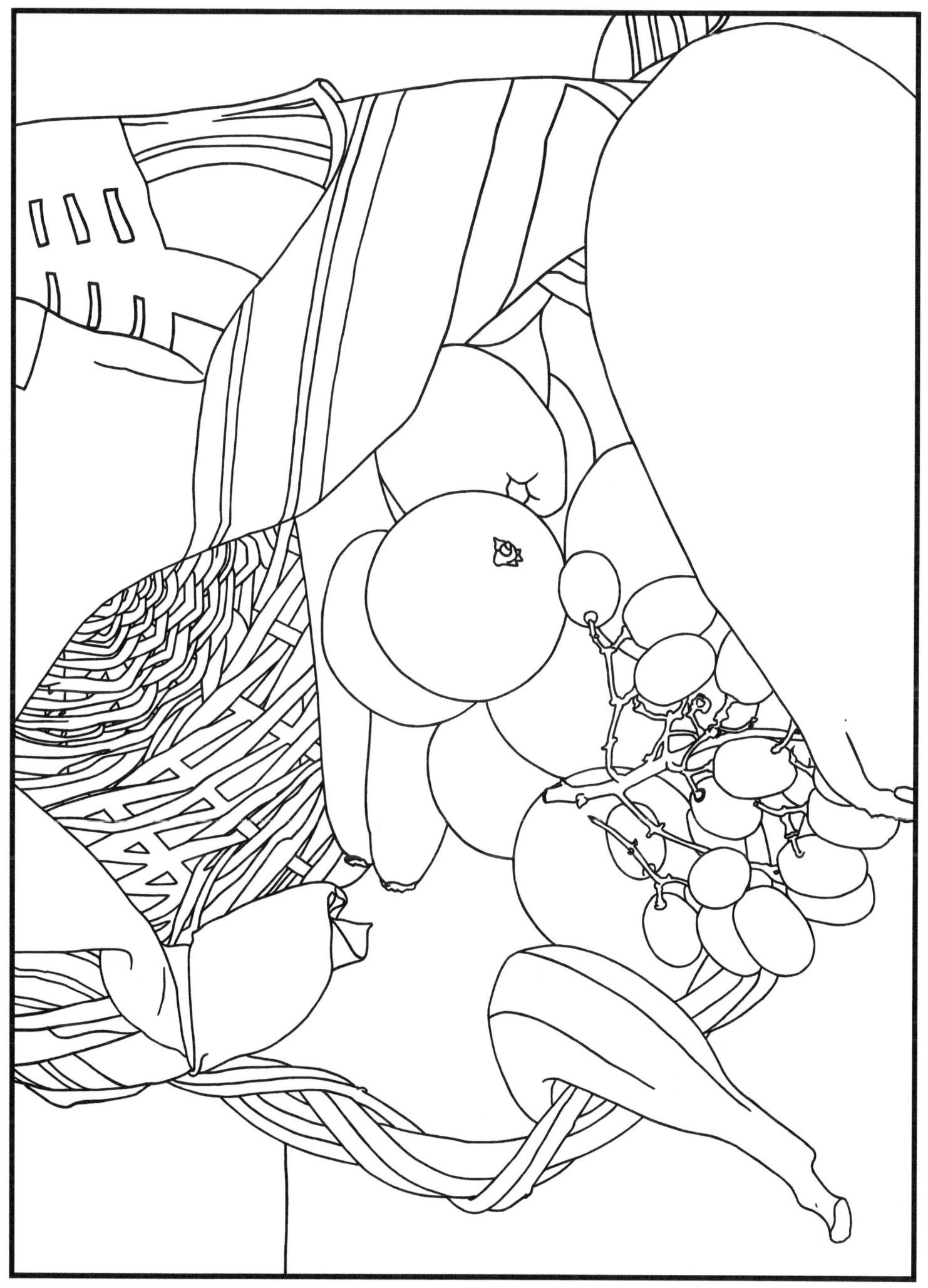

Fruit #4

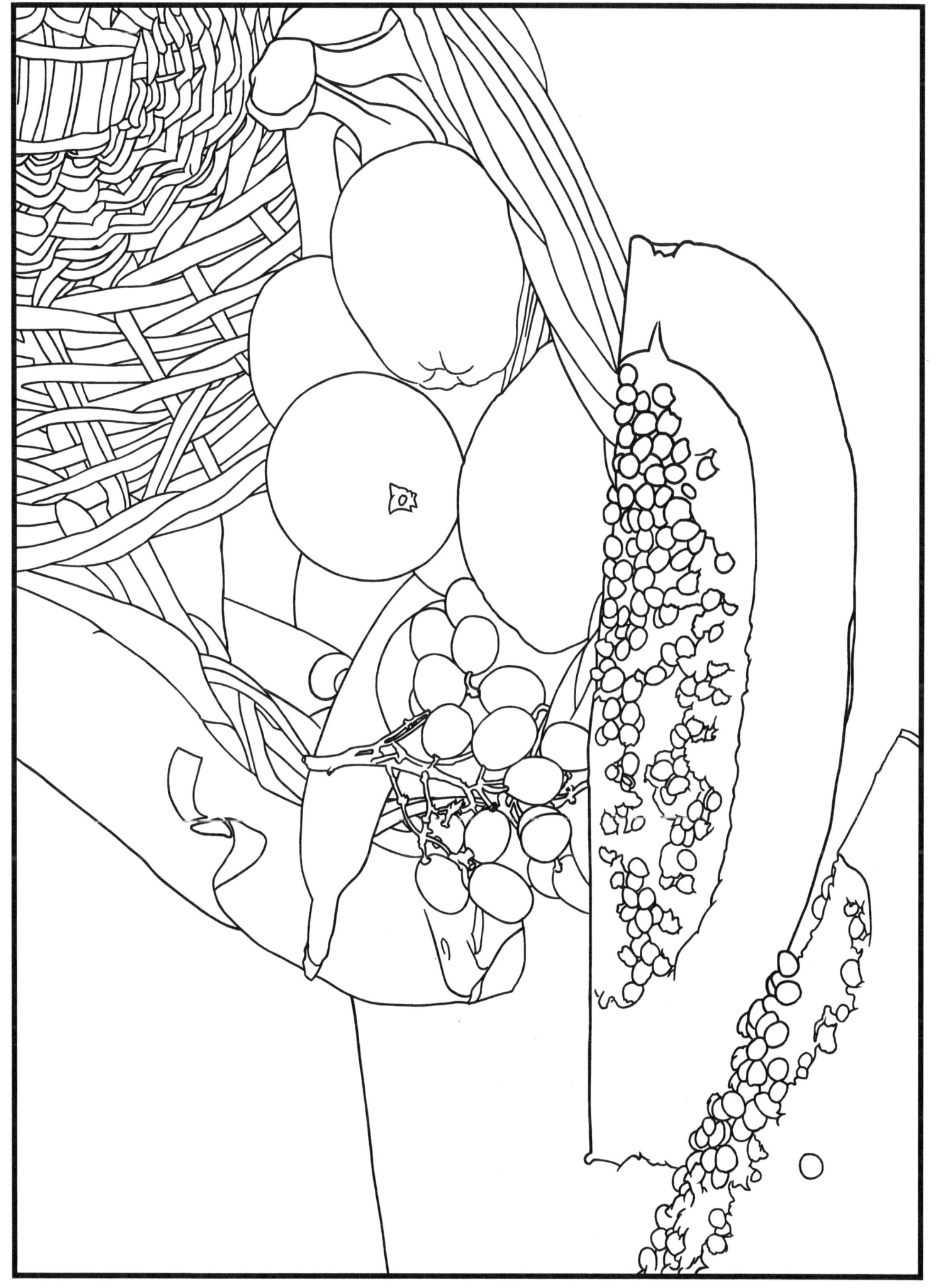

Fruit #5

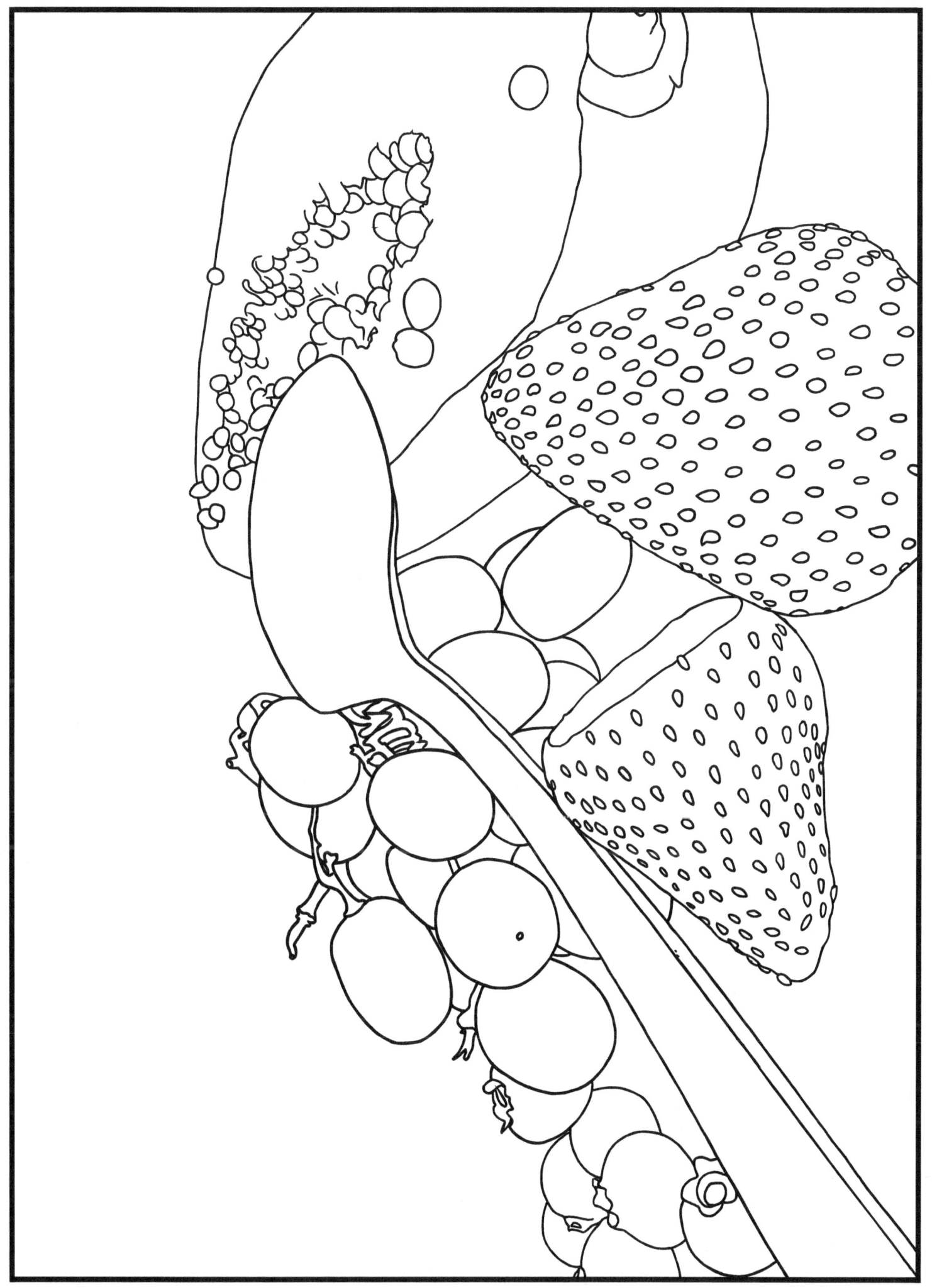

Fruit #6

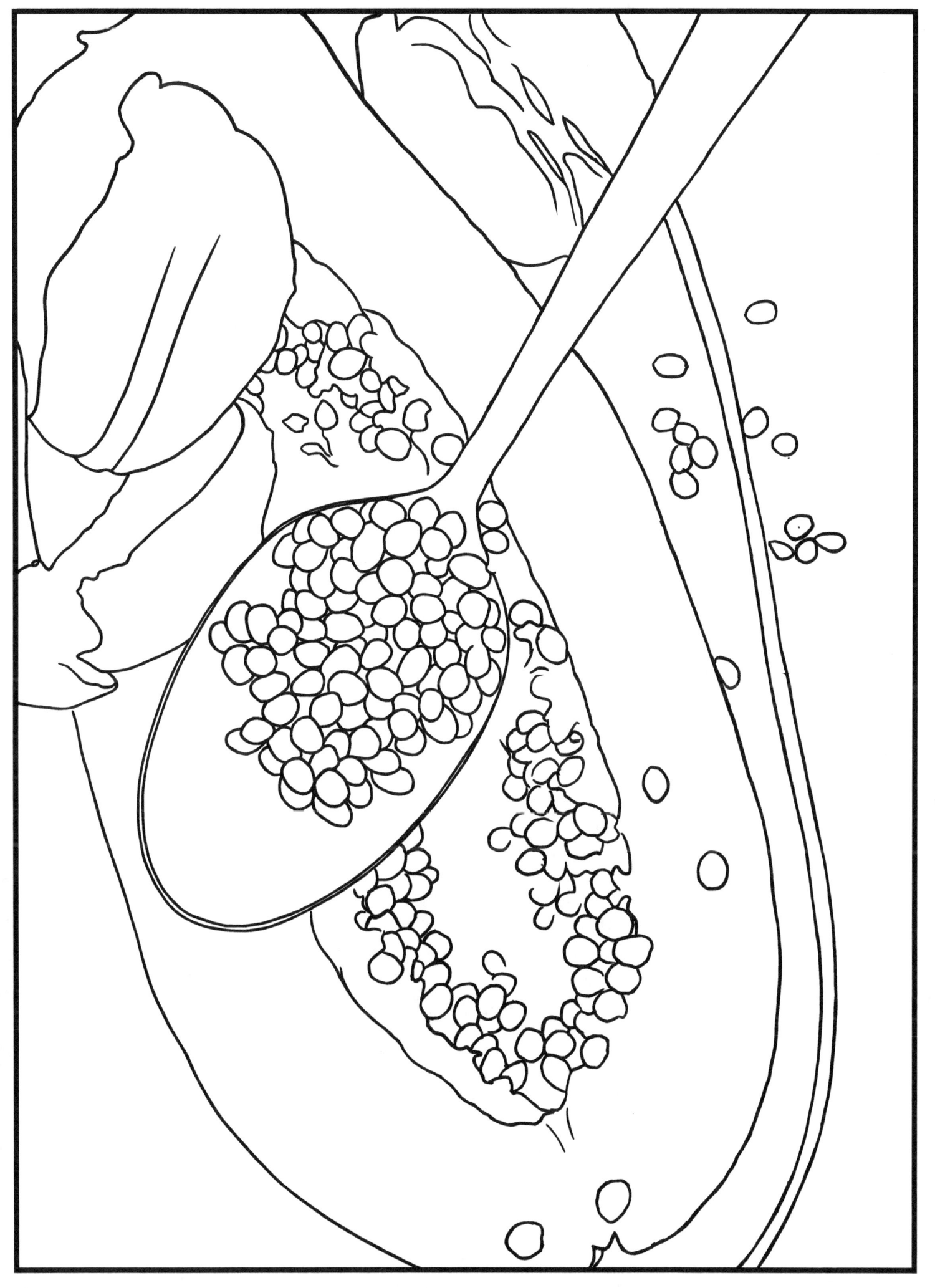

Seeds

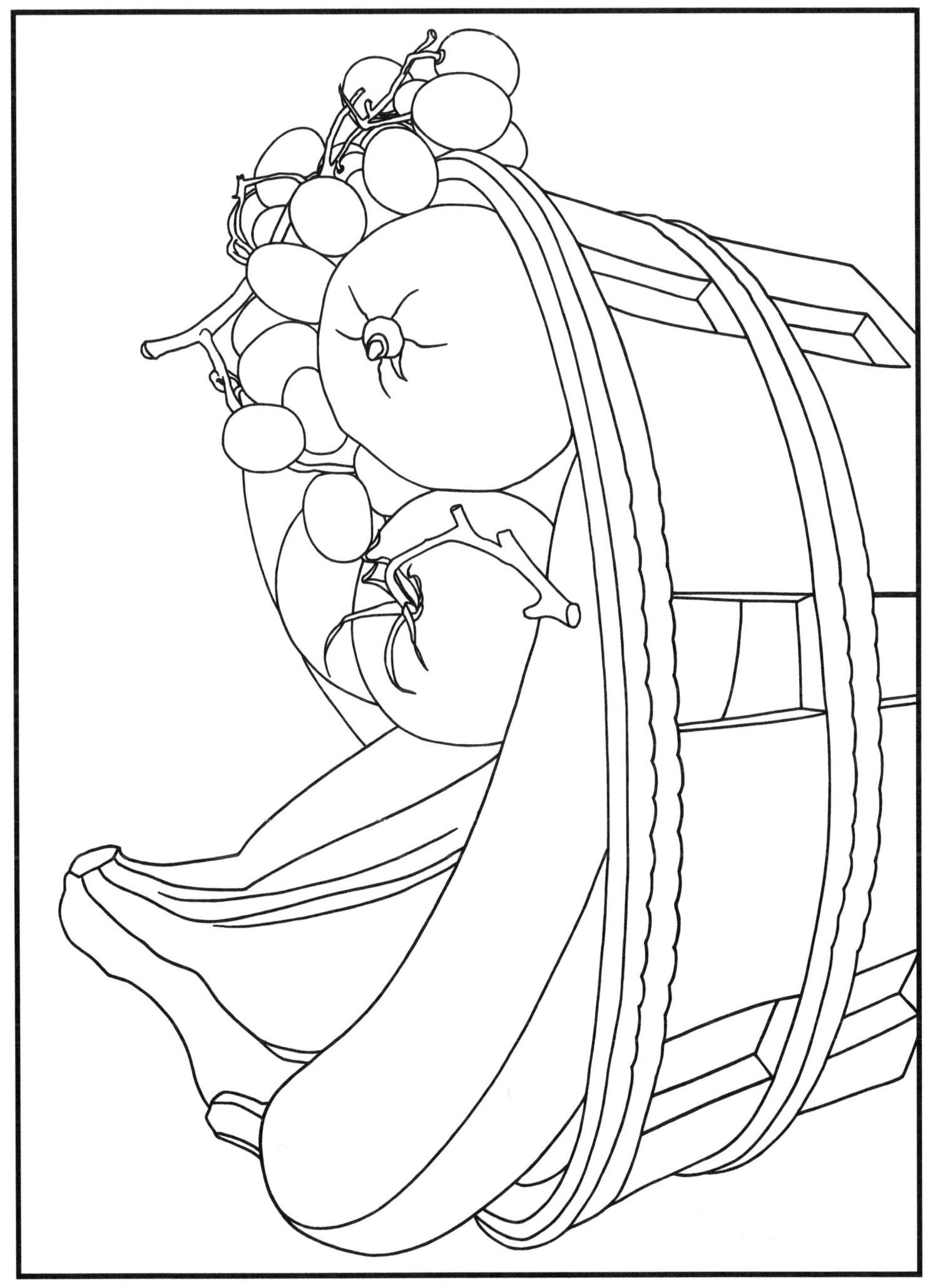

Fruit in Basket

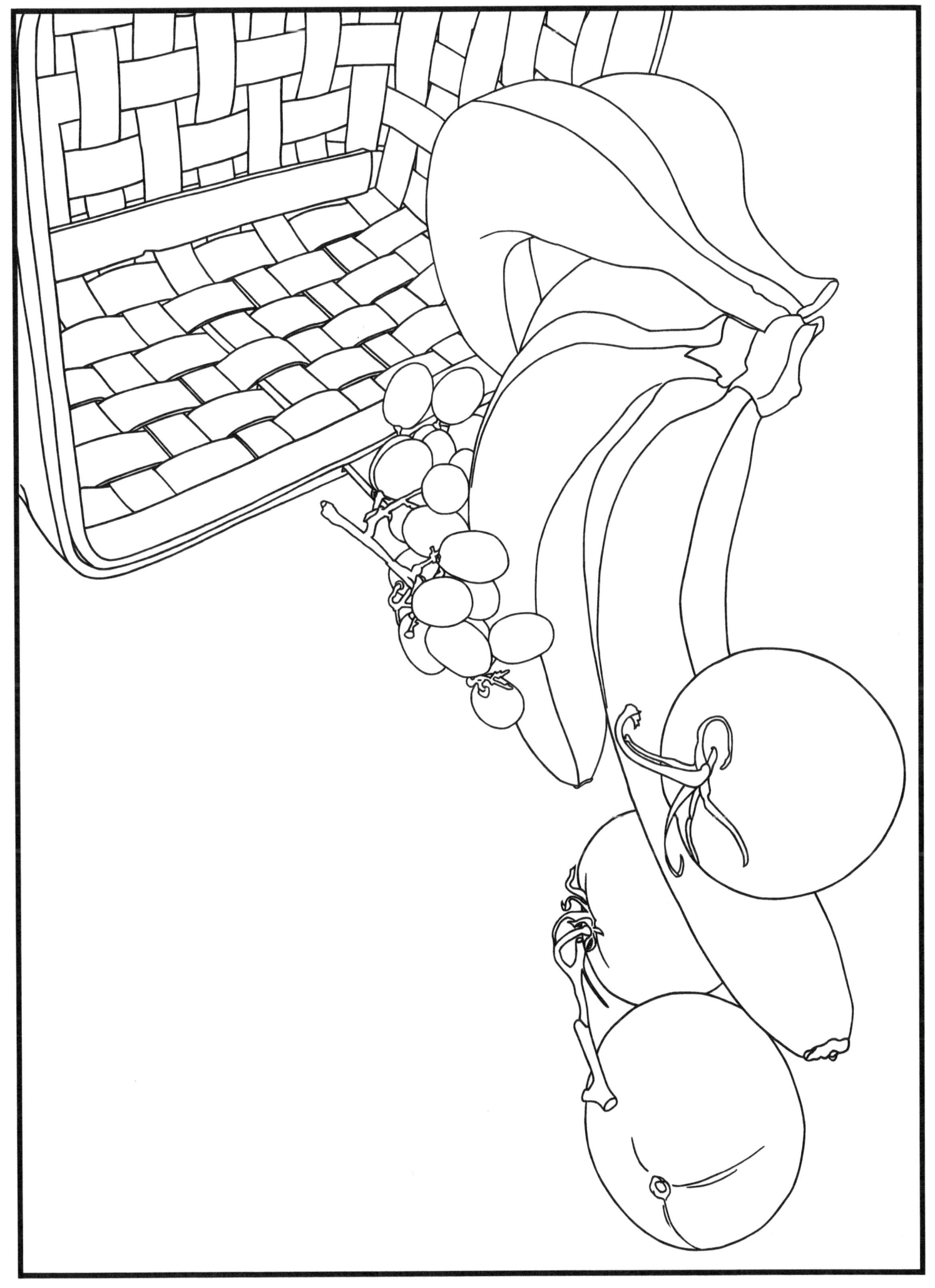

Fruit and Basket

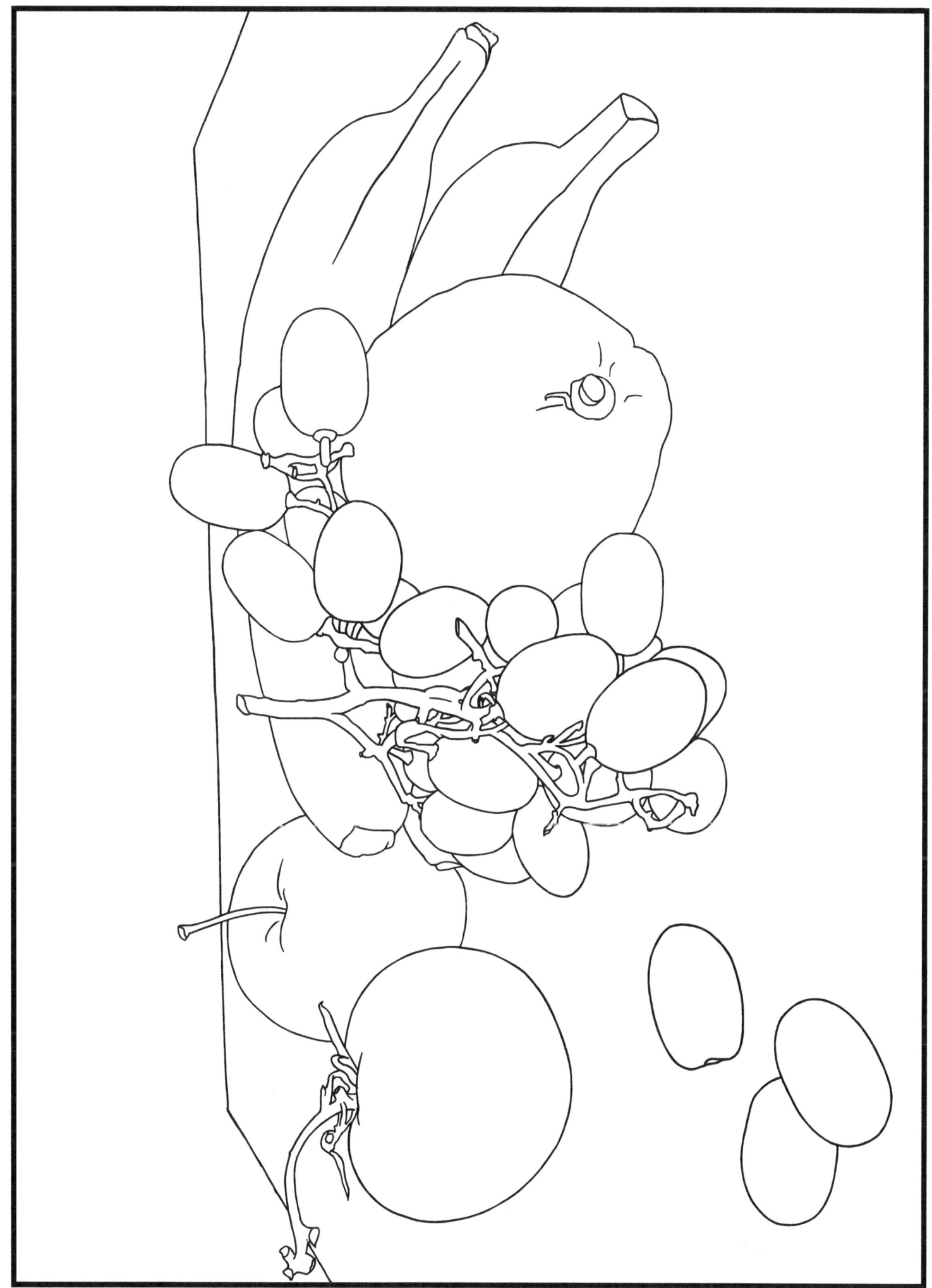

Fruit on Cutting Board

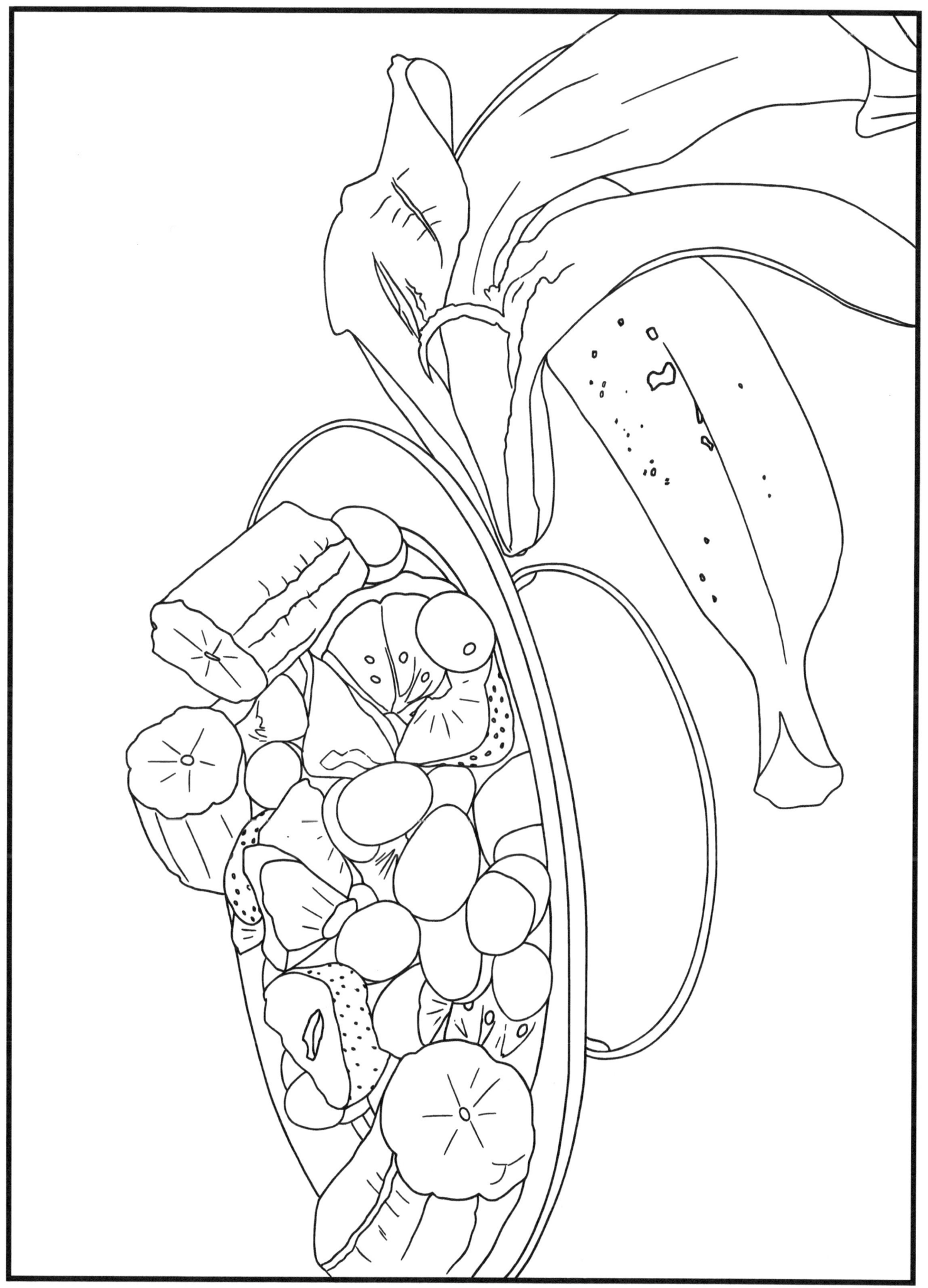

An A-peelin' Display

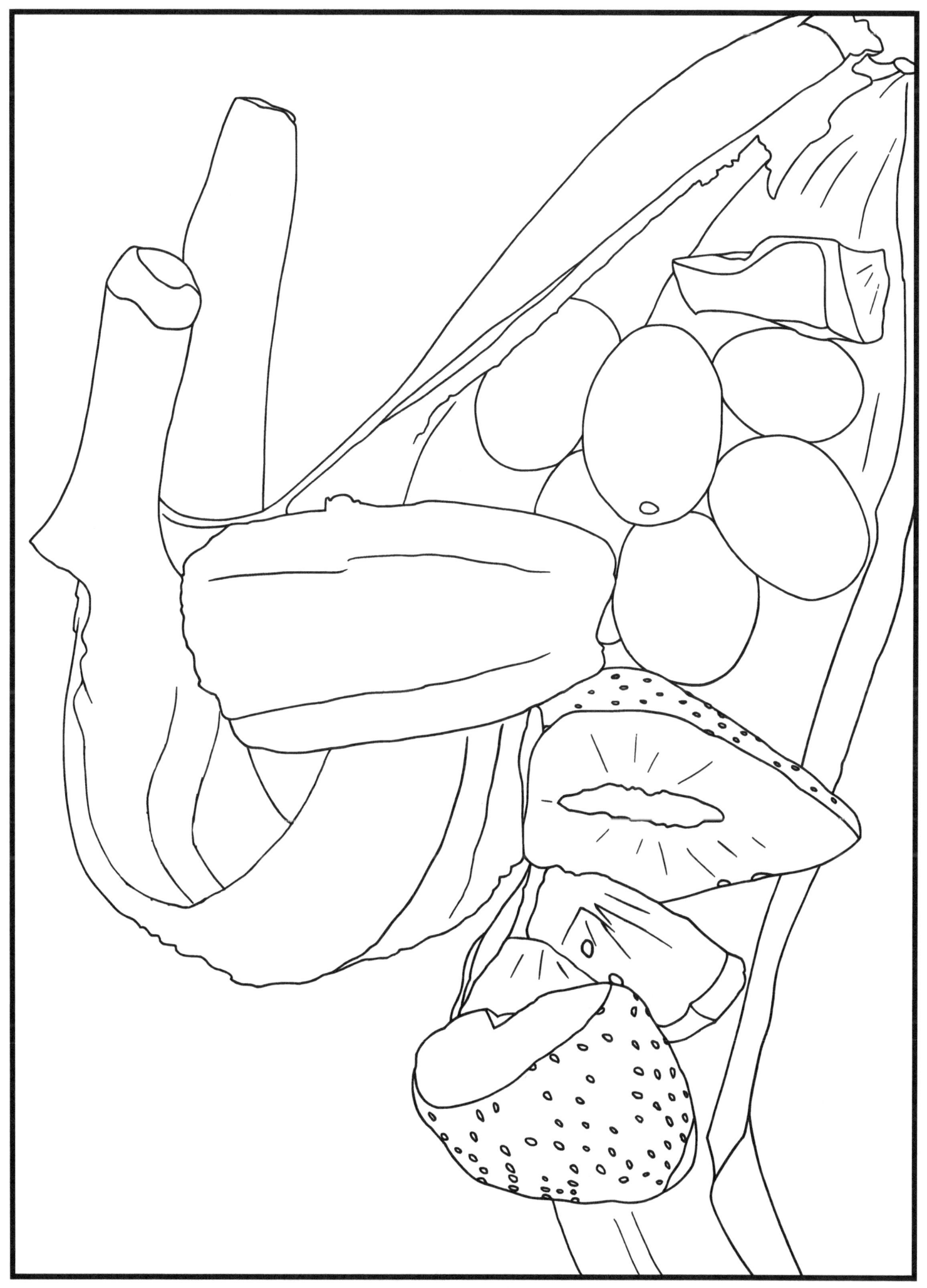

Banana Peel

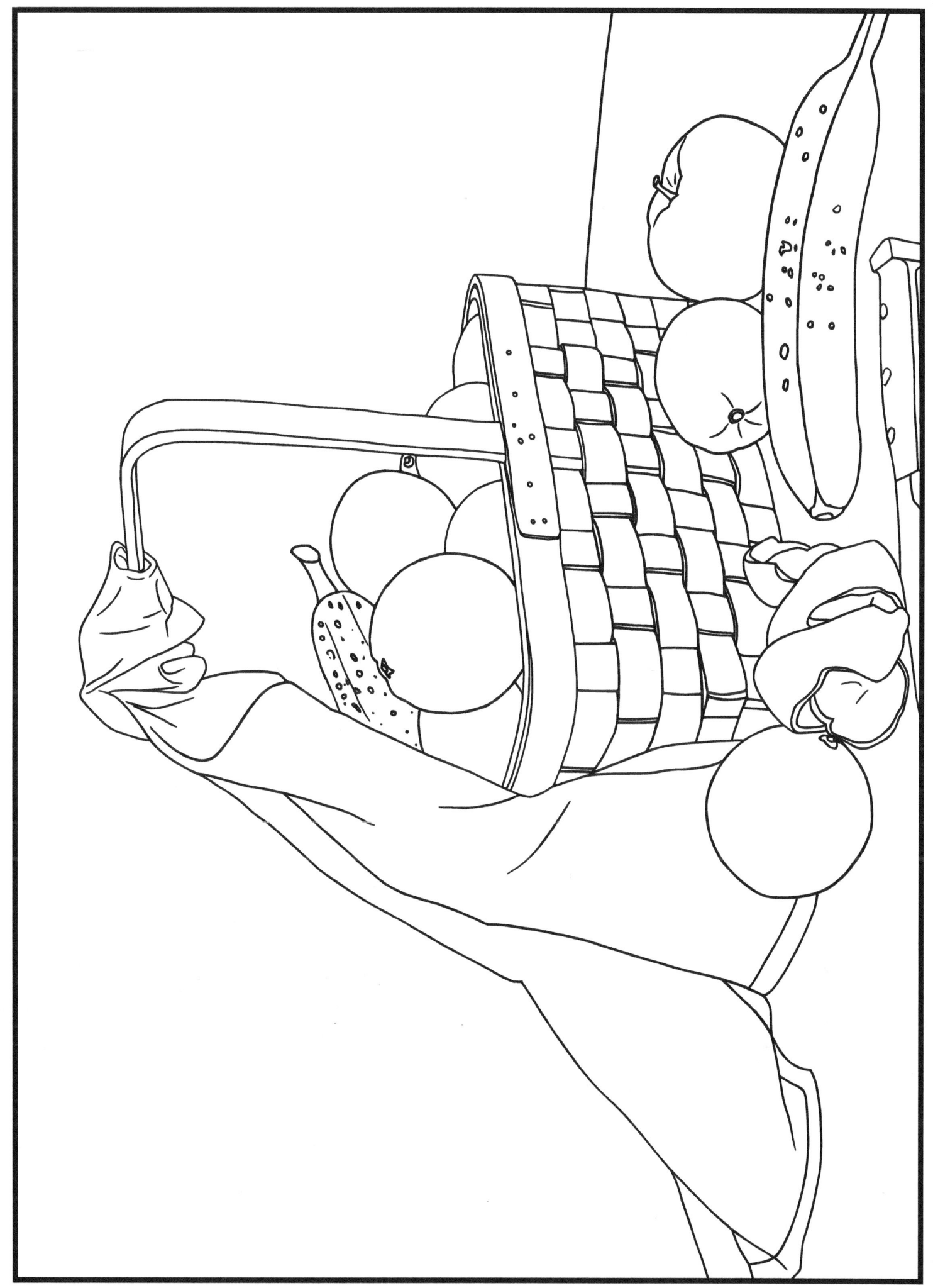

Picnic Basket

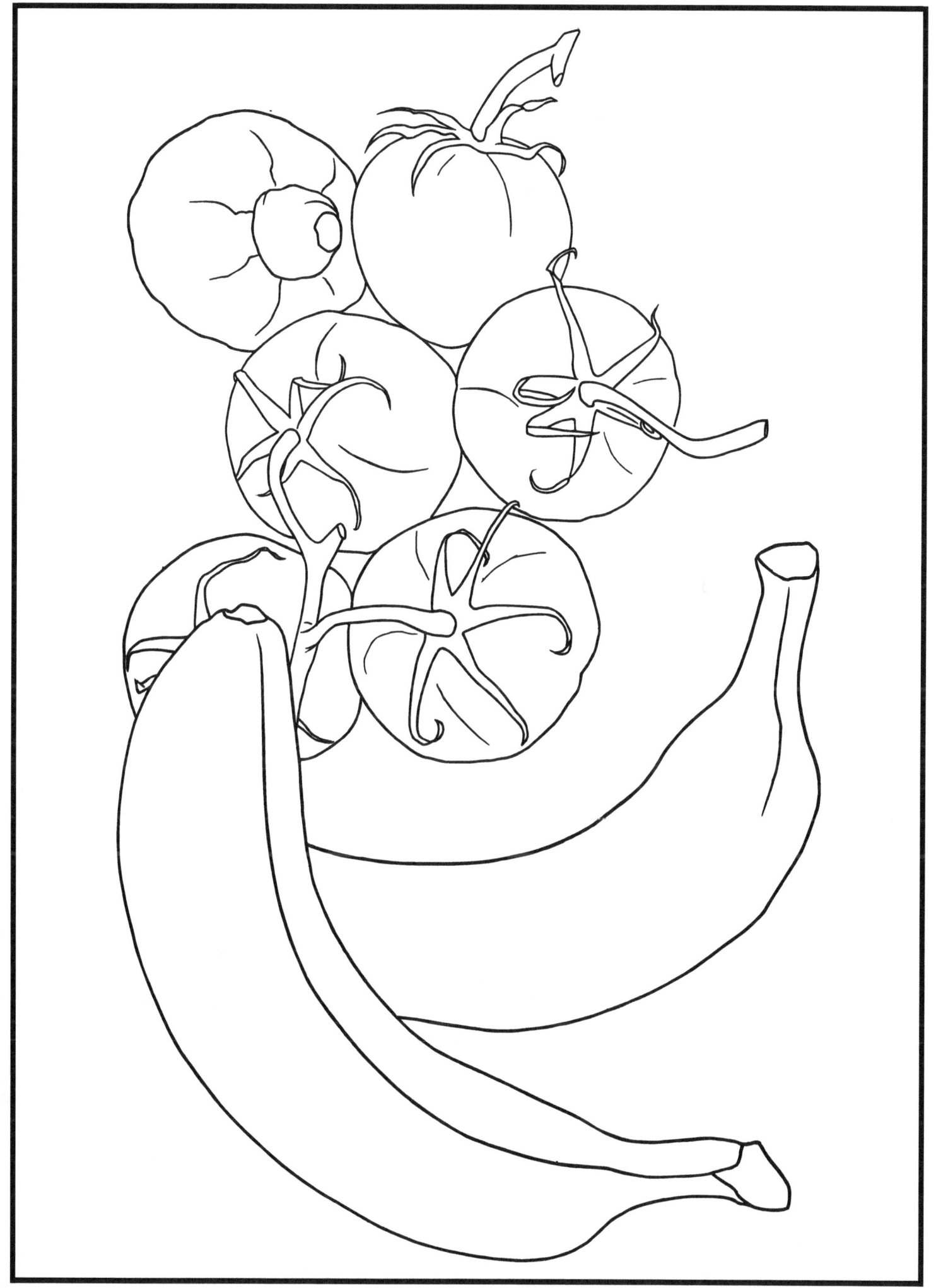

Yellow and Red

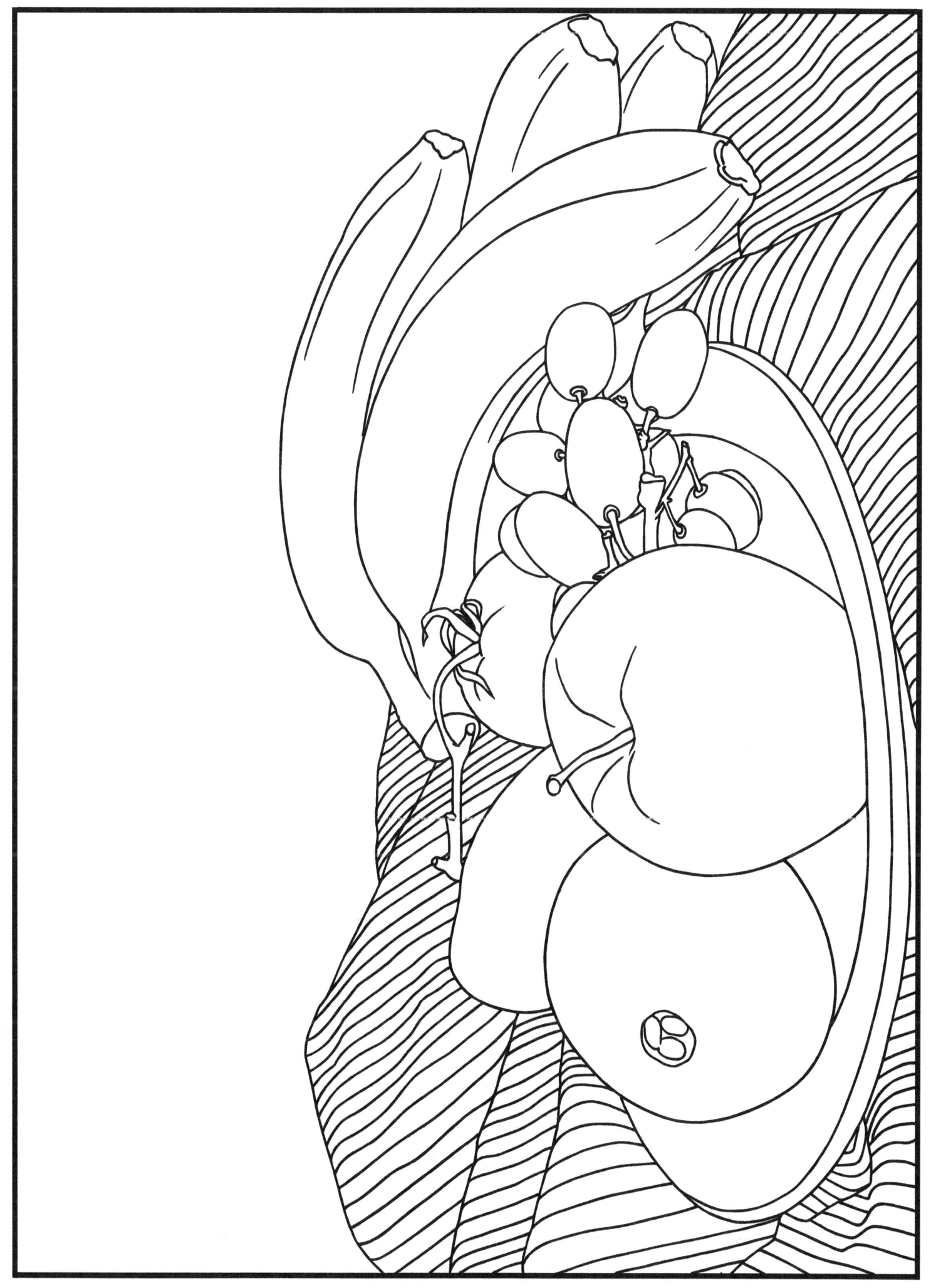

Apples, Grapes, and Bananas on Cloth

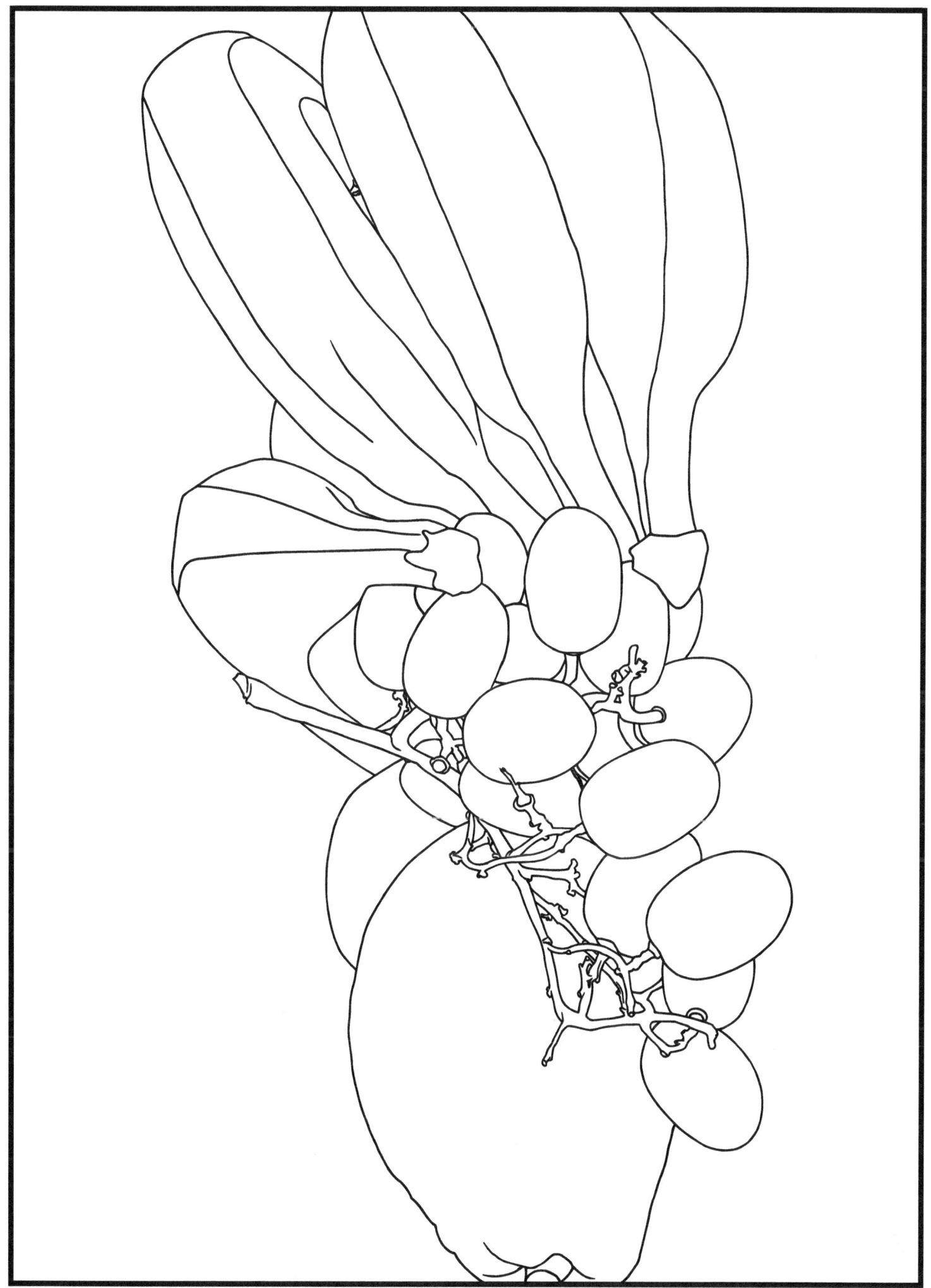

Bunches

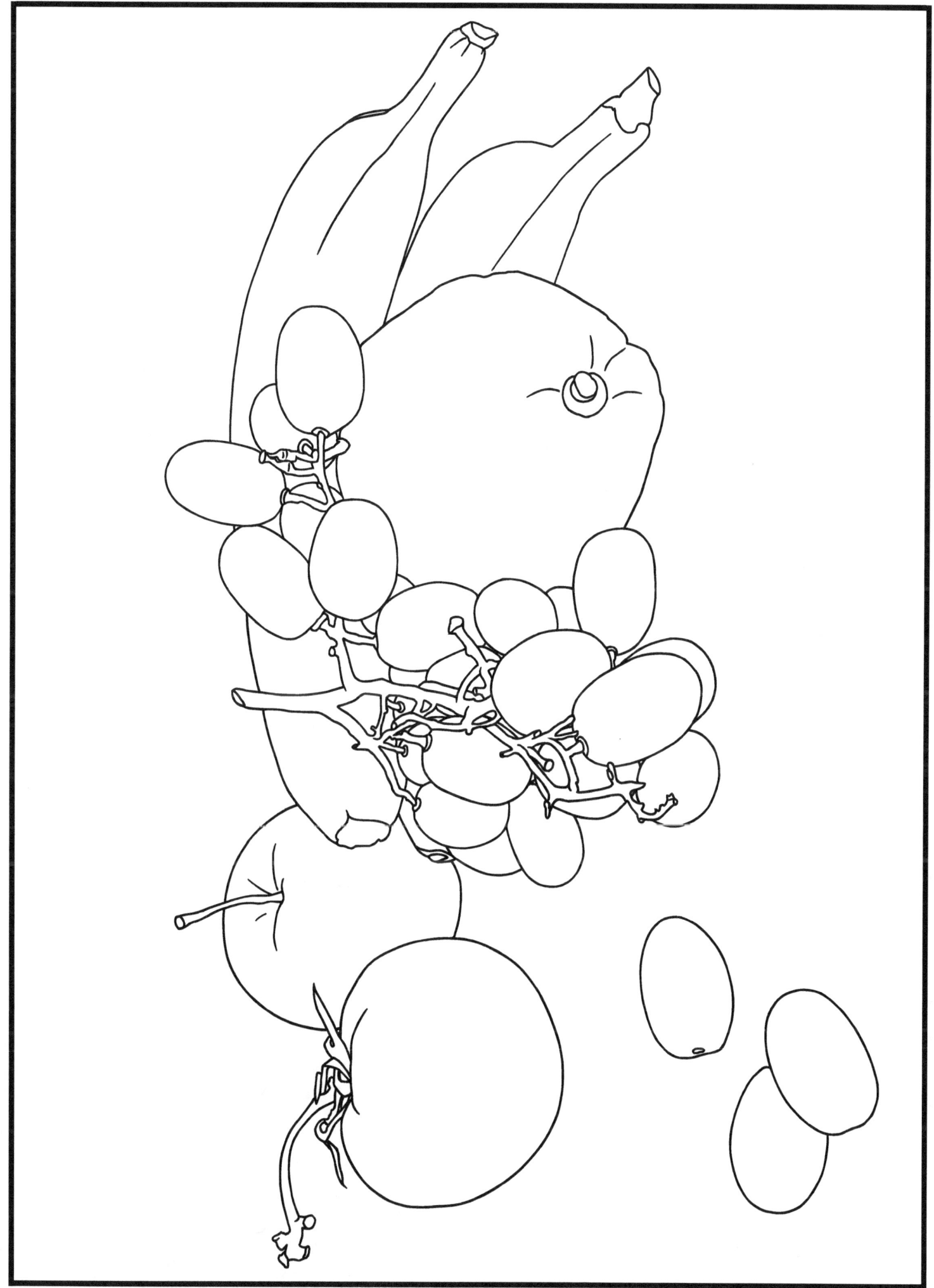

Tomatoes Are a Fruit Too

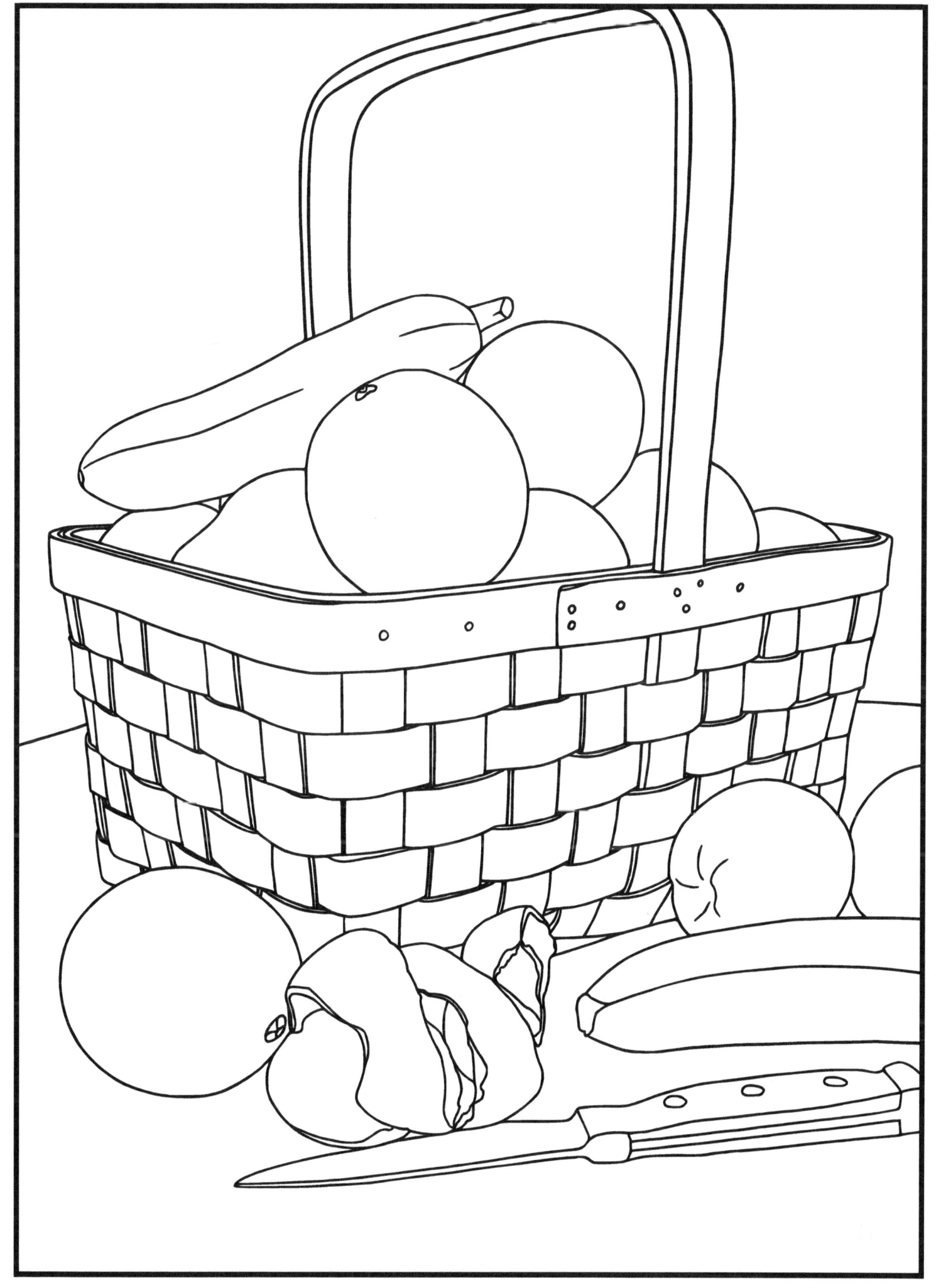

Basket Close-up

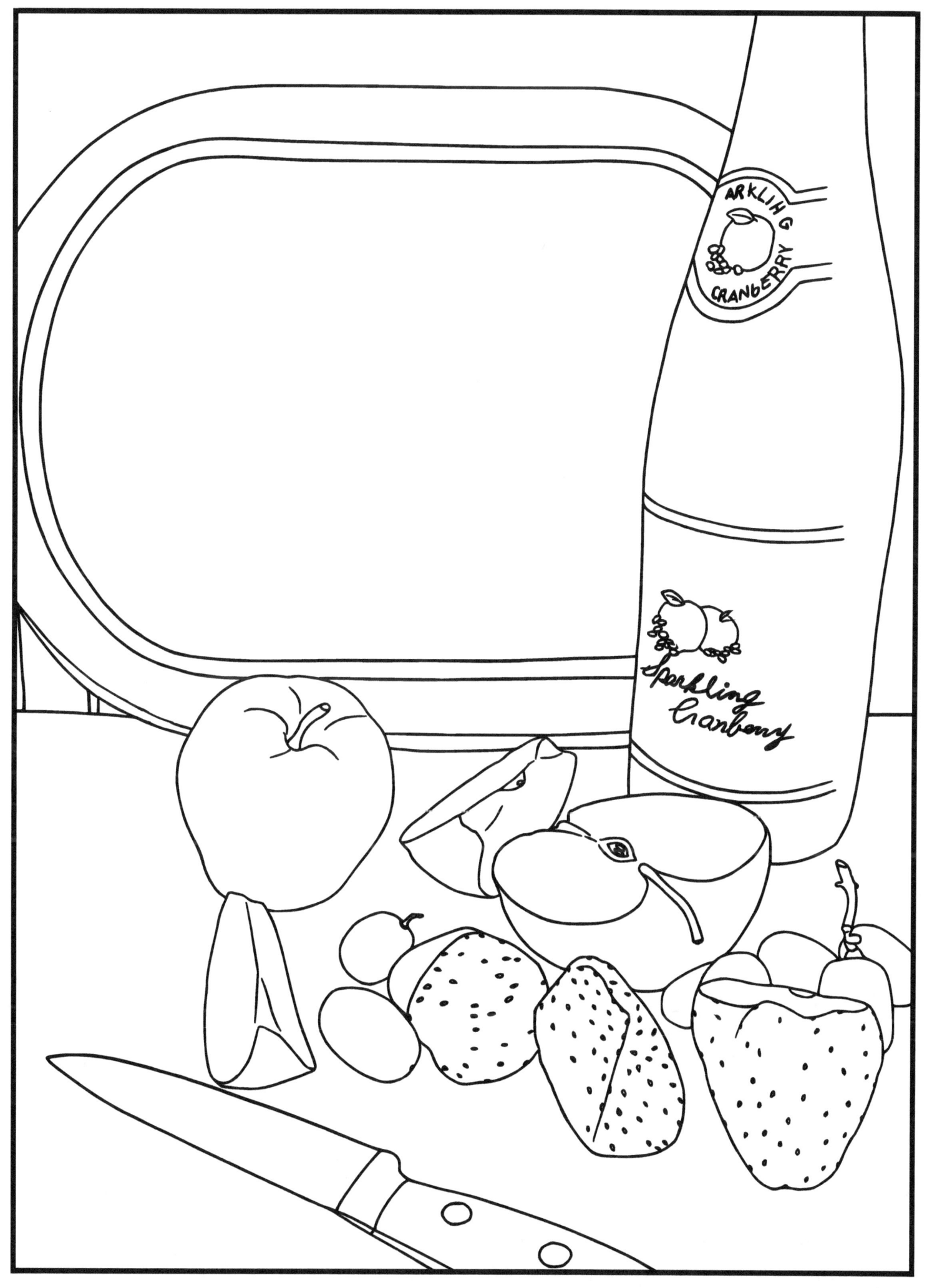

Sparkling Cranberry and Strawberries

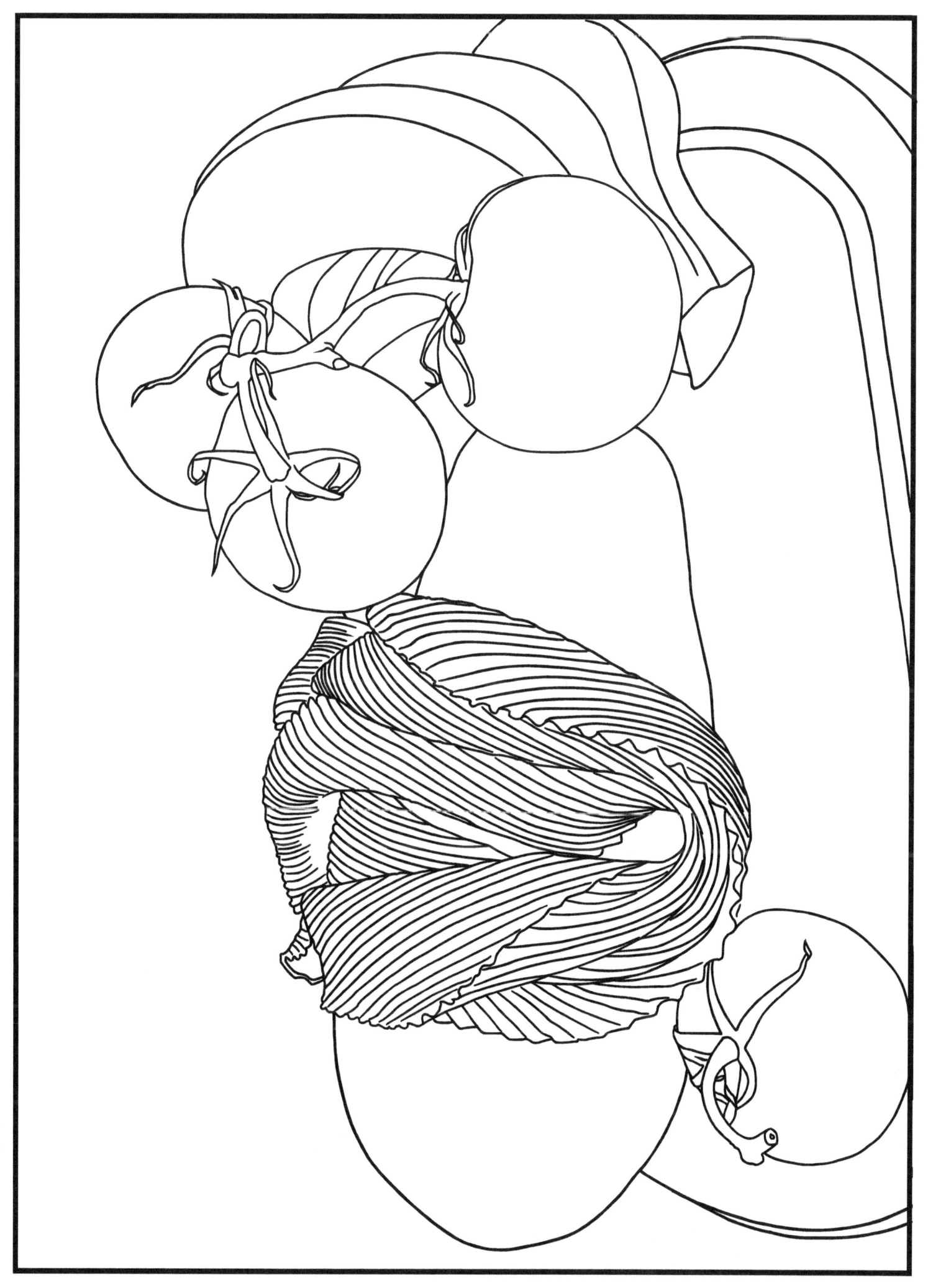

Cutting Board Arragement

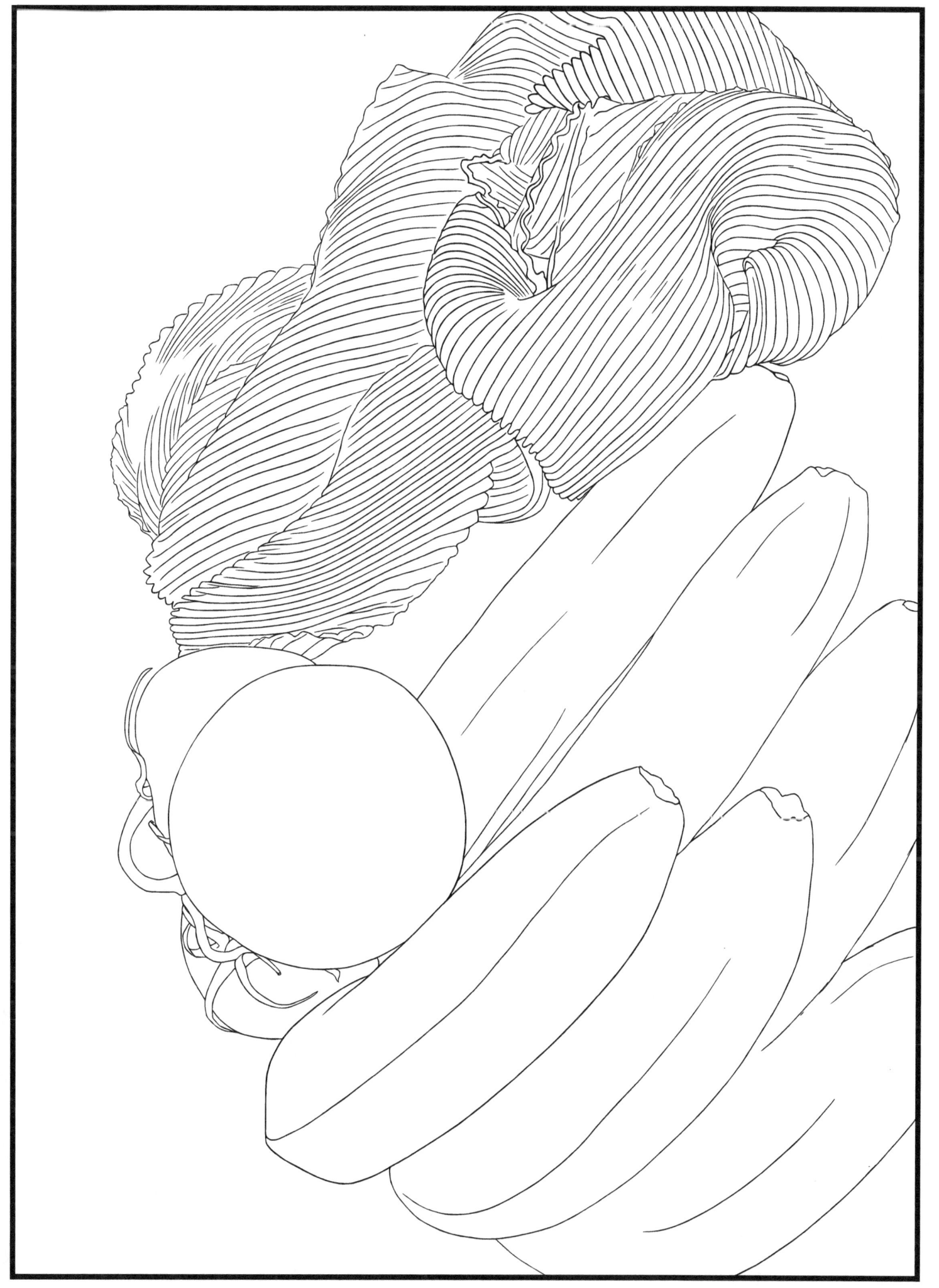

Bunches and Bundles

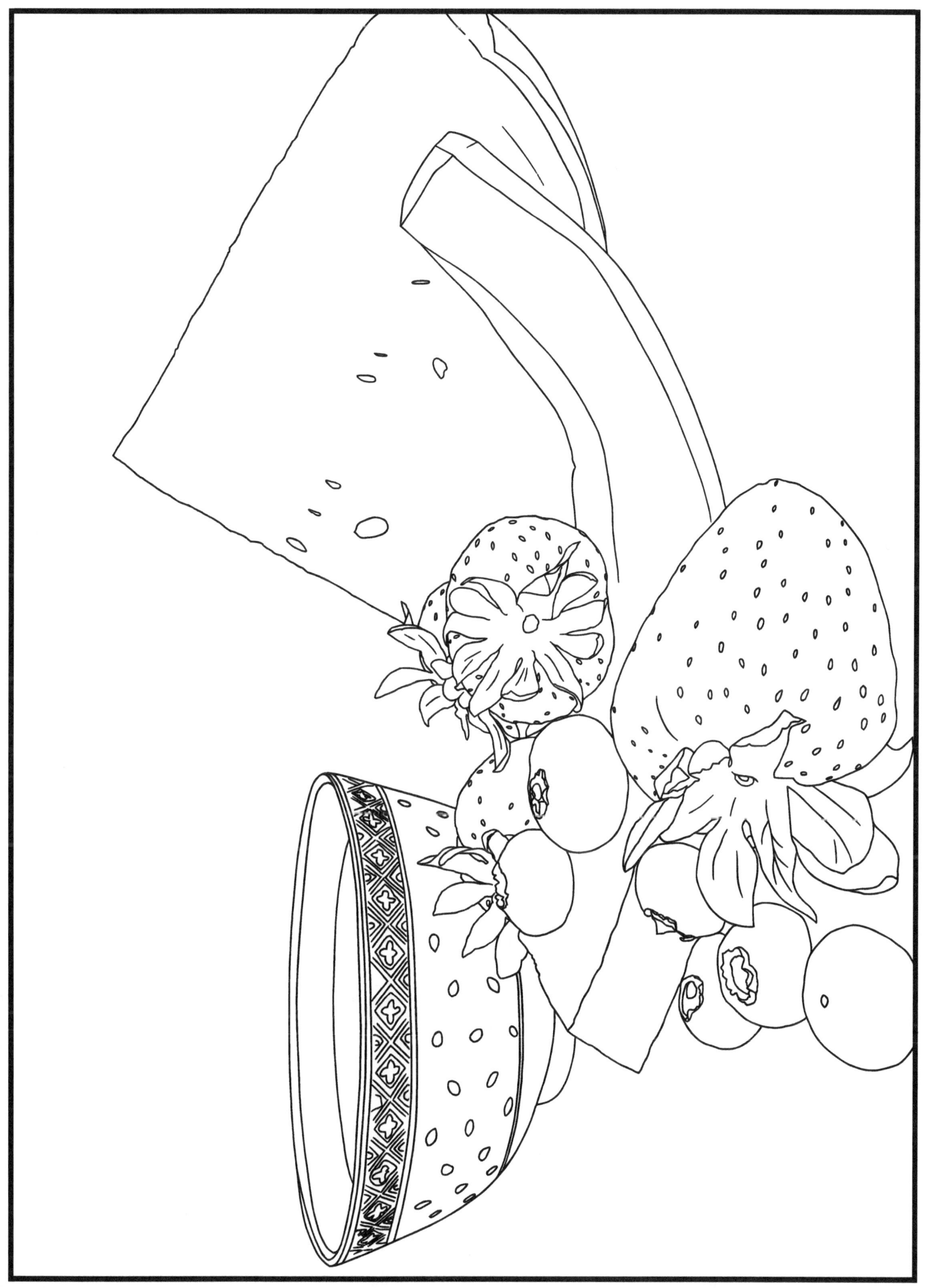

For a Summer's Day

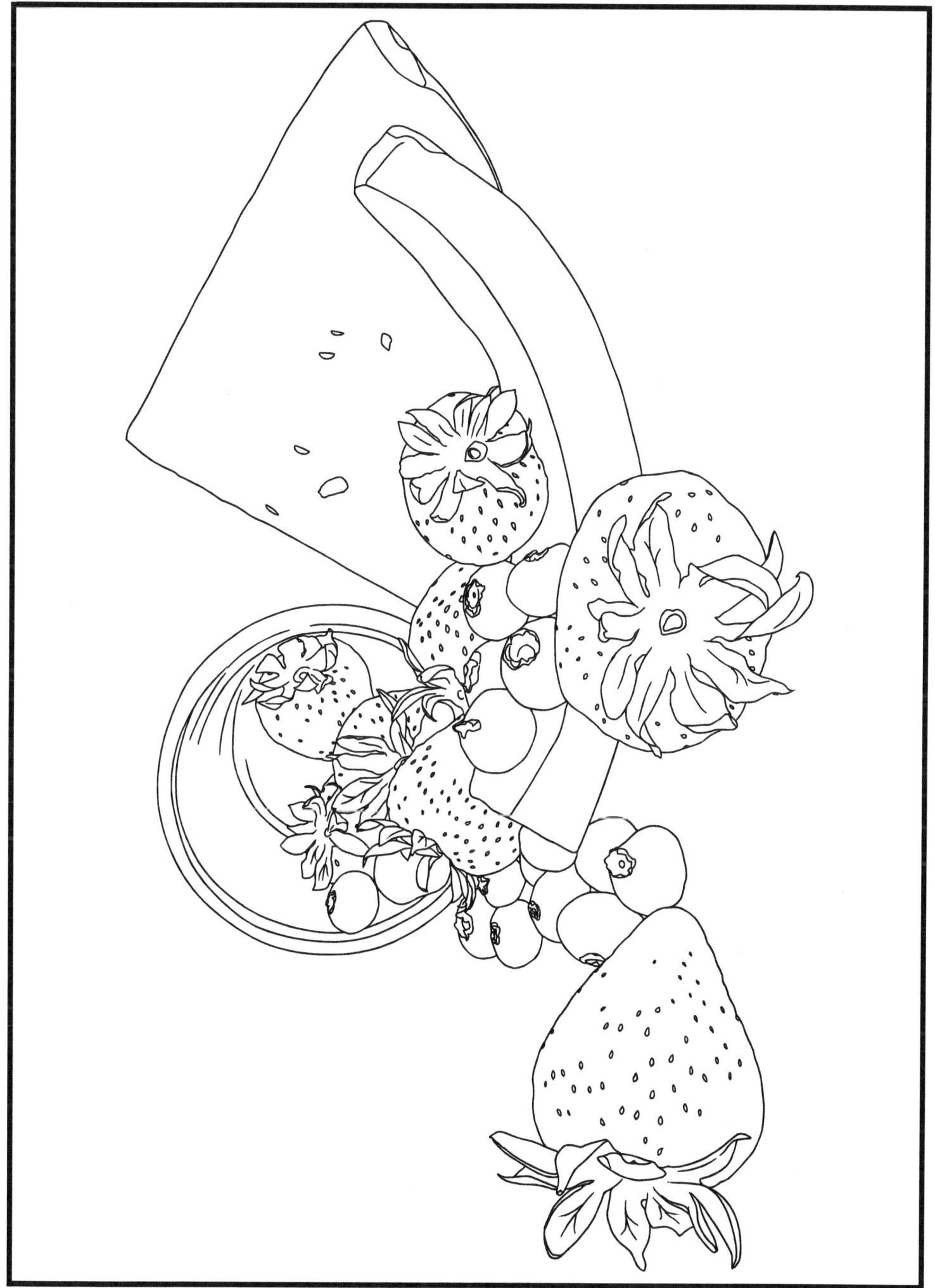

For Your Health

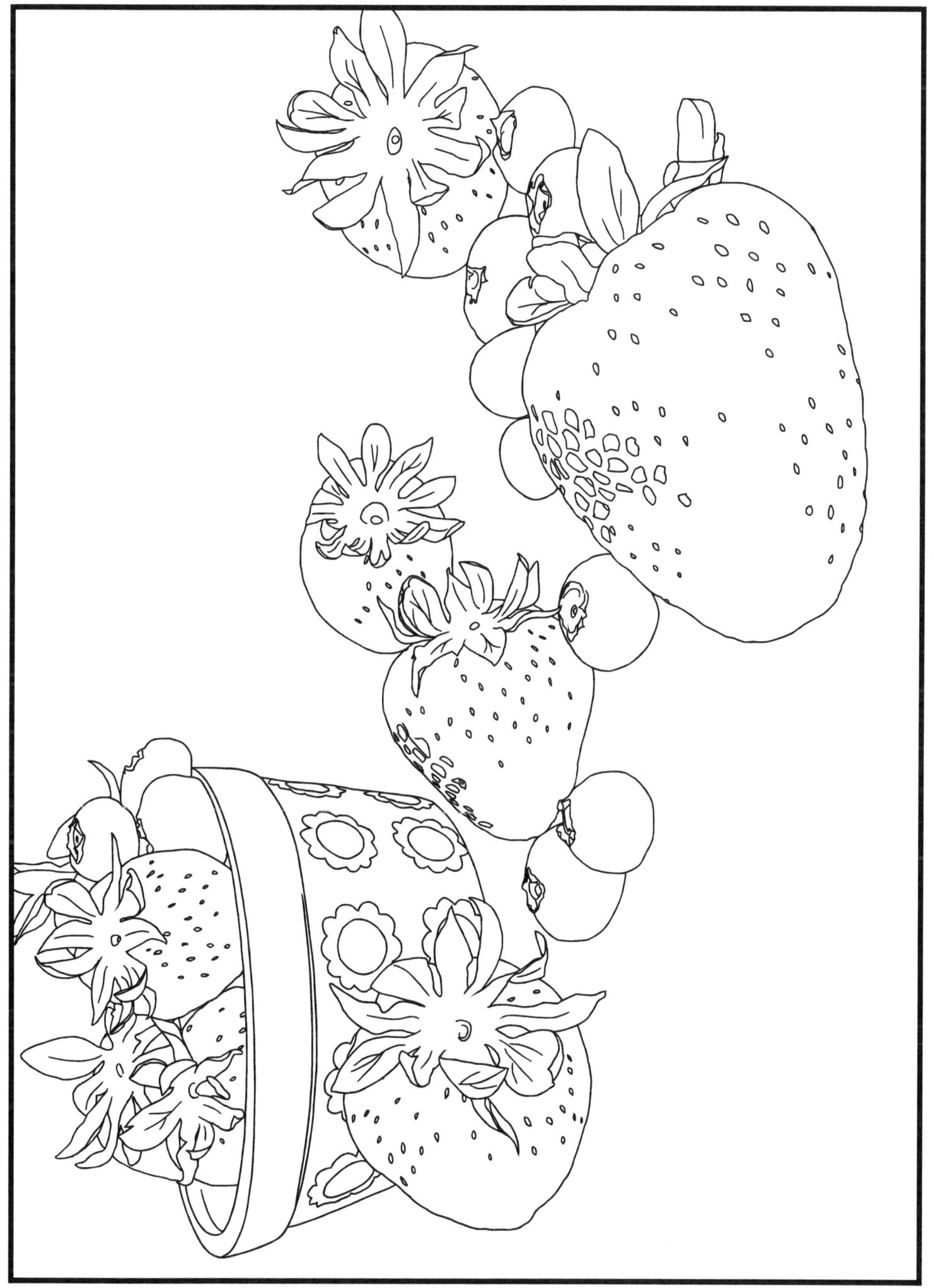

Strawberries Still Life

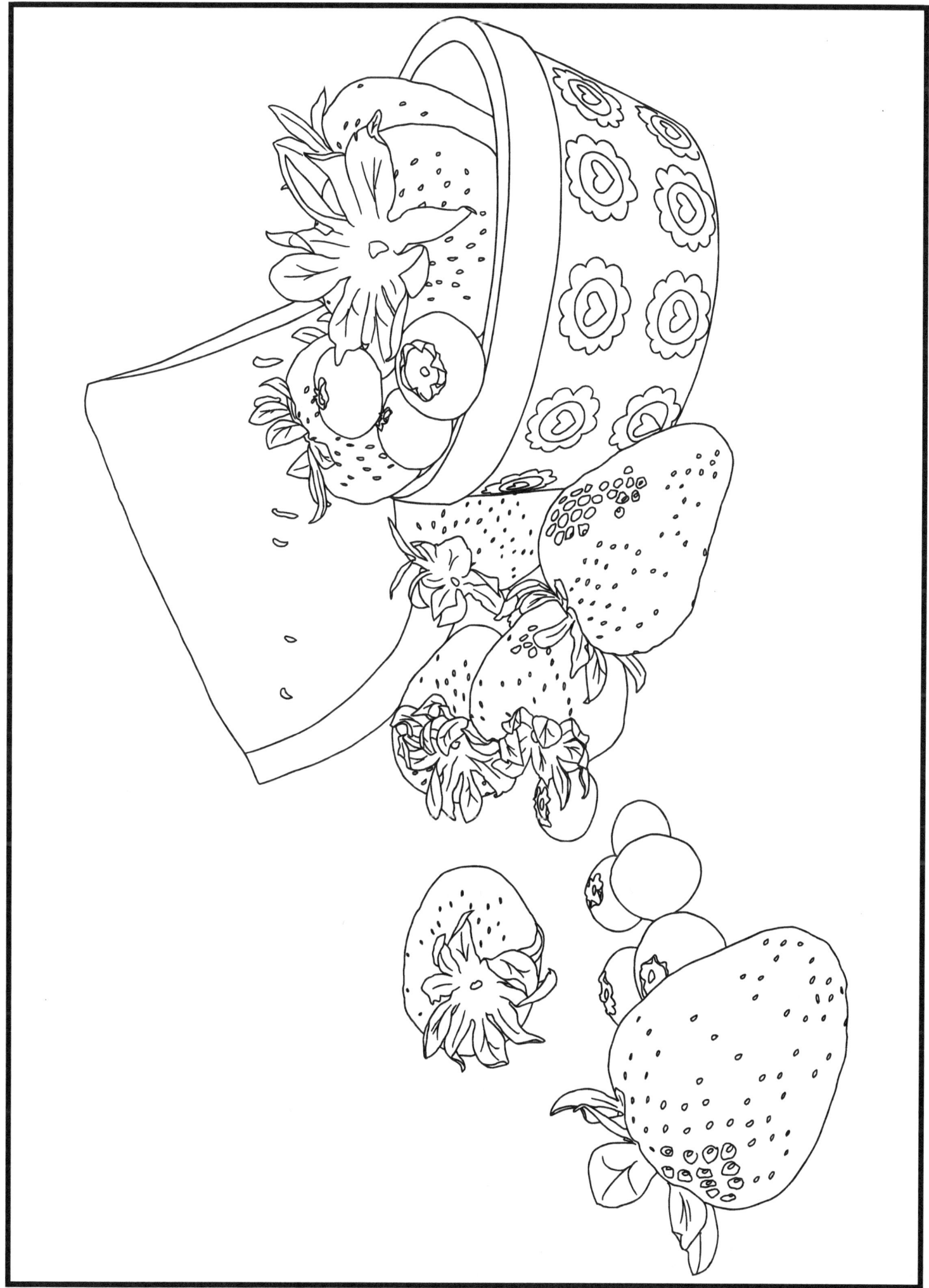

Berry Delicious

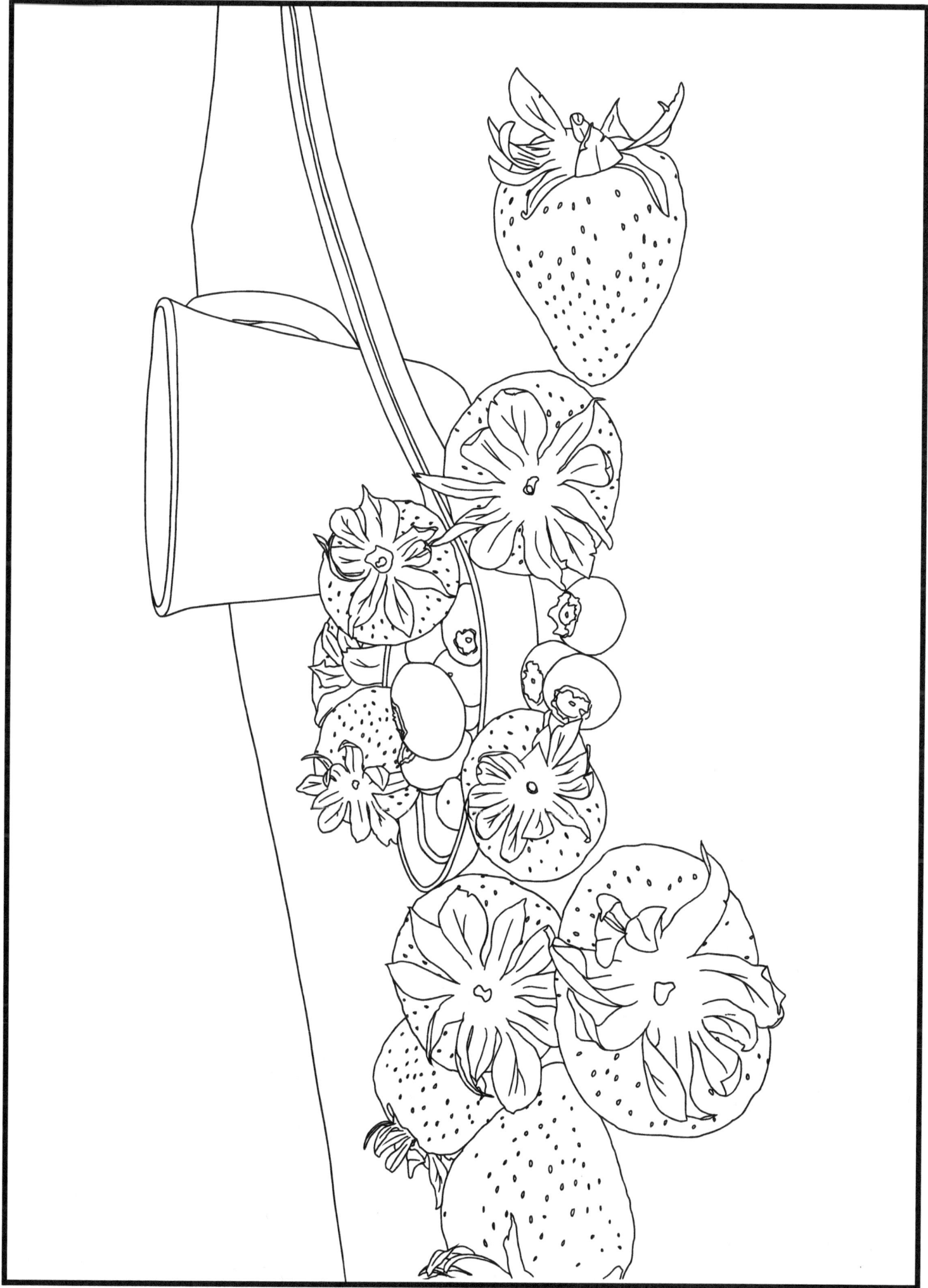

Chinese Spoon

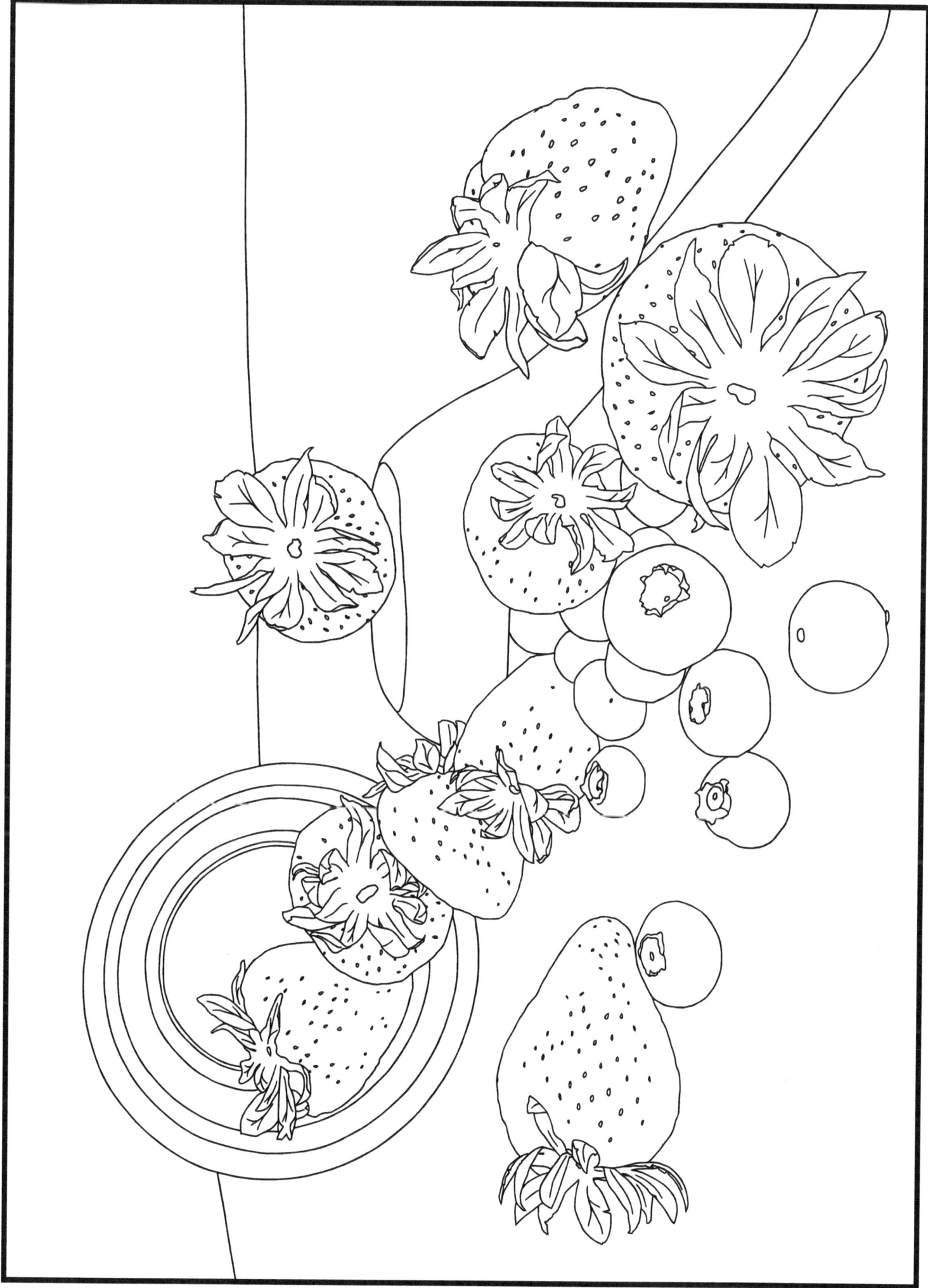

Berry Arrangement

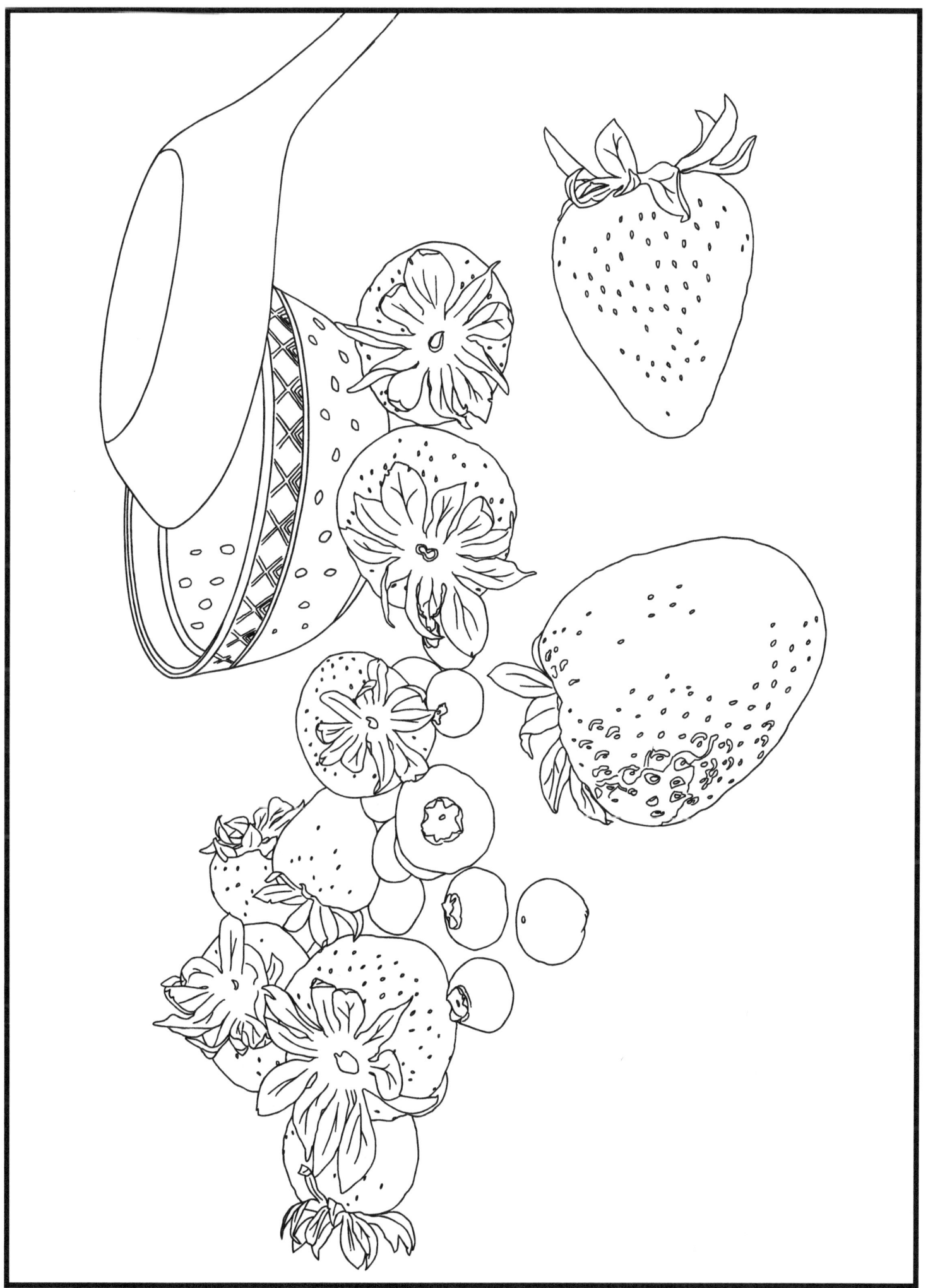

Berry Arrangement #2

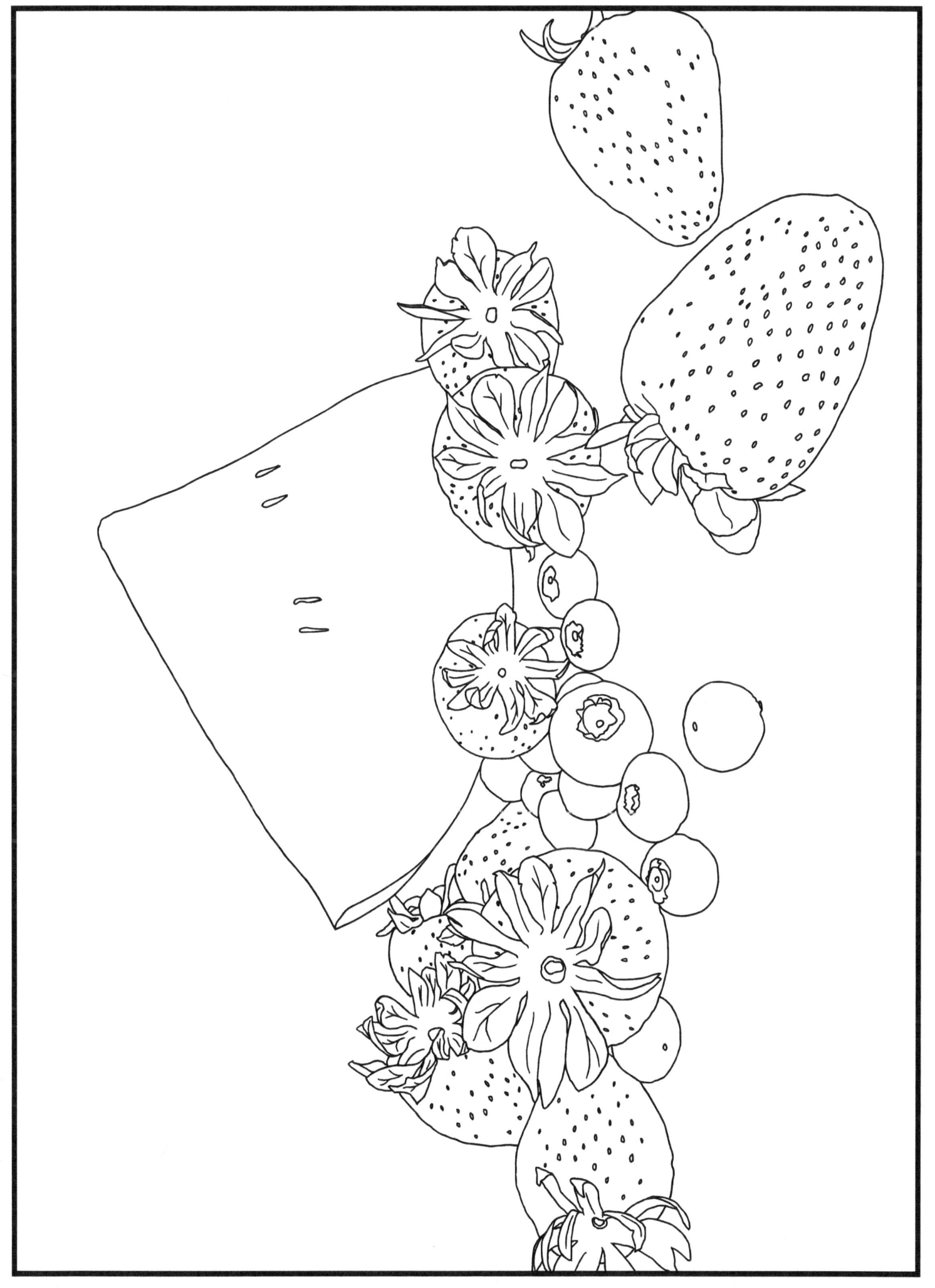

Berry Arrangement #3

Color Test Page

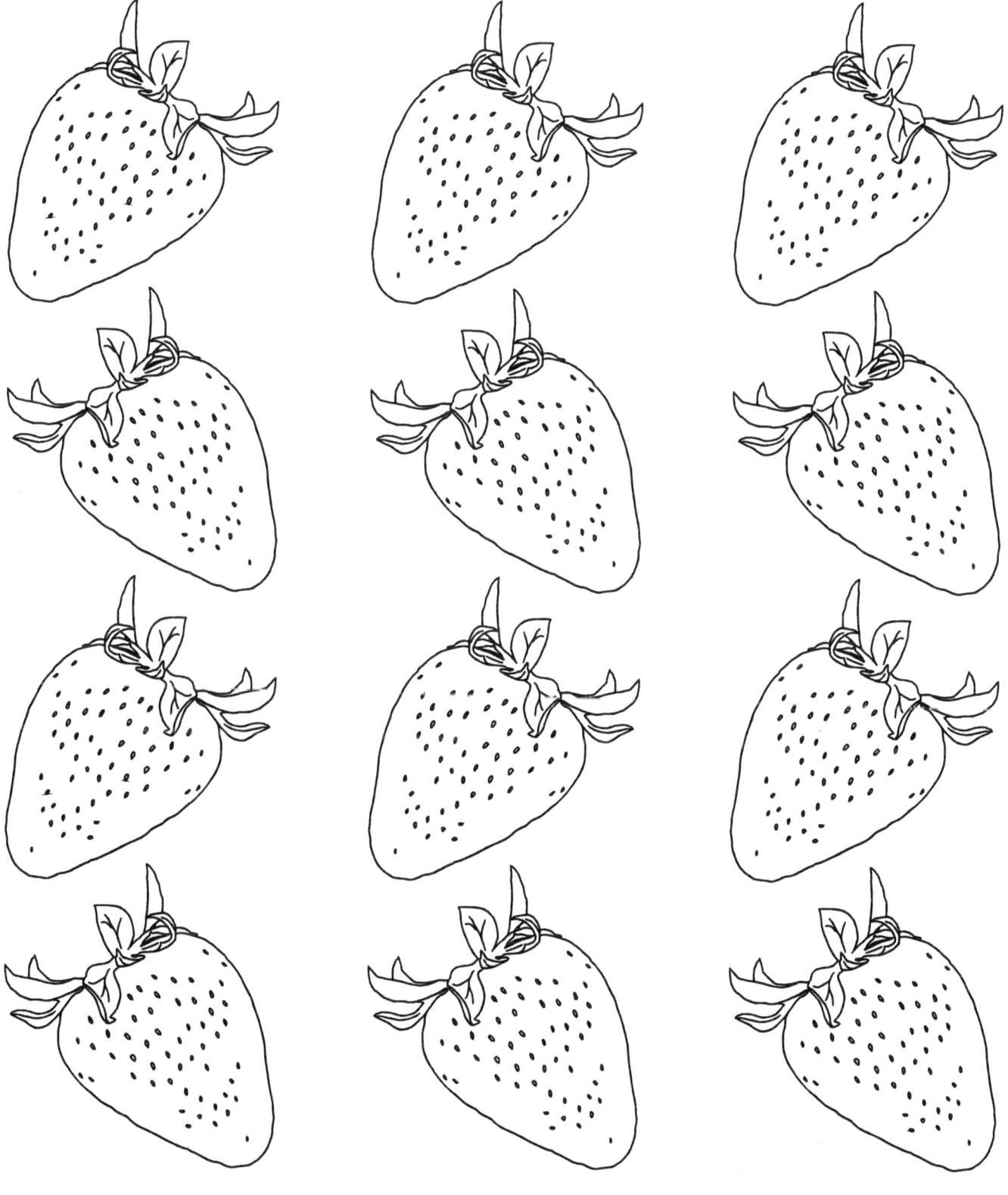

www.ingramcontent.com/pod-product-compliance
Lightning Source LLC
Chambersburg PA
CBHW062158220526
45470CB00009B/2859